A Travel Guide to World War II Sites in Italy

A Travel Guide to World War II Sites in Italy

Museums, Monuments, and Battlegrounds

ANNE LESLIE SAUNDERS

Travel Guide Press

Travel Guide Press
Charleston, South Carolina
www.travelguidepress.com

Design by Paul Rossmann Illustration Design

ISBN 1-4505-5612-4
Published 2010

The author thanks the following publishers for permission to quote from these works: Johnson & Alcock, from Douglas Orgill's *The Gothic Line;* Lonely Planet, from Eric Newby's *Love and War in the Apennines*; McFarland & Company, from Robert B. Ellis's *See Naples and Die: A World War II Memoir of a United States Army Ski Trooper in the Mountains of Italy*; University of Missouri Press, from Eugenio Corti's *The Last Soldiers of the King*; University of Nebraska Press, from Ernie Pyle's *Brave Men*, and *The Fighting 36th Historical Quarterly*, from that publication.

Photographs courtesy of the U.S. National Archives, Library and Archives Canada, and the Frank J. Davis World War II Photograph Collection at Southern Methodist University.

Front cover: Allied soldiers advance along mountain roads in Italy, April 1945.
Back cover: An American soldier stands in a bomb-shattered church near Salerno, September 1943.

Table of Contents

Acknowledgments 11

Transportation Tips 12

Hotels 13

Chapter 1: Introduction: Italy 1914–1945 15

Chapter 2 Map 22

Chapter 2: Cassino and Caserta 23
  Historical Summary 23
  Sites within Cassino 24
    Abbey of Monte Cassino 24
    Polish Cemetery 26
    Historiale 26
    Cassino War Cemetery *(Commonwealth)* 26
    Memorials in the Center of Cassino 27
  Sites near Cassino 27
    History Memorial Park of San Pietro Infine 27
    Italian War Cemetery at Mignano Monte Lungo 28
    French War Cemetery in Venafro 29
    German Military Cemetery at Caira 29
    36th Division Monument and Peace Bell Tower 29
    Cassino War Memorial 30
  Caserta 30
    Royal Palace of Caserta 30
    Caserta War Cemetery *(Commonwealth)* 30

Chapter 3 Map 32

Chapter 3: Pomezia, Anzio, Nettuno, and Borgo Faiti 33
  Historical Summary 33
  Pomezia: German Military Cemetery 34
  Anzio 34
    Beachhead Museum 34
    Anzio War Cemeteries *(Commonwealth)* 35
    Memorials at the Anzio Harbor 36
  Nettuno 36
    Sicily-Rome American Cemetery and Memorial 36
    Monuments in the Center of Nettuno 37
    Museum of the Allied Landing 38
  Borgo Faiti: History Museum, La Piana delle Orme 38

Chapter 4: Rome (Part A)..39
  Historical Summary...39
  Sites...40
    Basilica of Saint Lawrence outside the walls..............................40
    St. Paul's Gate...41
    Ostiense Train Station 41
    Rome War Cemetery *(Commonwealth)*.....................................42
    Protestant Cemetery...42
    Jewish Museum and the Great Synagogue 42

Chapter 5: Rome (Part B)..45
  Historical Summary...45
  Sites...46
    Via Rasella..46
    History Museum of the Liberation 47
    Ardeatine Graves..49
    Basilica of Saint John Lateran...49
    Memorials in the Via Veneto Neighborhood 50
    Villa Torlonia *(Mussolini's Home)*..50

Chapter 6 Map..52
Chapter 6: From Ortona to Rimini, and on toward Bologna.................53
  Historical Summary...53
  From Ortona to Rimini 55
    Museum of the Battle of Ortona...55
    Memorials in Piazza Plebiscito 55
    Commonwealth War Cemeteries...56
      Sangro River
      Moro River
      Ancona
      Gradara
      Montecchio
    Gothic Line Museum at Montegridolfo..56
    War Memorials in Gemmano...57
    Coriano War Cemetery *(Commonwealth)* 57
  From Rimini toward Bologna...58
    Piazza Tre Martiri...58
    Rimini Gurkha War Cemetery *(Commonwealth)* 58
    Aviation Museum 58

Commonwealth War Cemeteries 59
   Cesena
   Forlì
   Faenza
A Walk through Imola 59

Chapter 7 Map 60

Chapter 7: Sites between Florence and Imola 61
Historical Summary 61
Florence 63
   Museum of Jewish Art and History and the New Synagogue 63
   Bridges over the Arno River 63
   Florence War Cemetery *(Commonwealth)* 64
   Florence American Cemetery 64
From Florence to Imola 65
   War Museum at Scarperia 65
   Monuments near the Giogo Pass 65
   German Military Cemetery at Traversa 65
   Santerno War Cemetery at Coniale *(Commonwealth)* 66
   War Museum in Castel del Rio 66
   Monuments on Battle Mountain 66
   Vestiges of War in Tossignano 67
A Walk through Imola 67
   From Piazza Matteotti to Chiesa del Carmine 67
   The Fortress 69
   Documentation Center for the Resistance 69

Chapter 8: Lucca and Western Tuscany 71
Sites 71
   Gothic Line Fortifications at Borgo a Mozzano 71
   Sant'Anna di Stazzema National Park of Peace 72

Chapter 9 Map 74

Chapter 9: Sites between Lucca and Bologna 75
Historical Summary 75
Sites 76
   Riva Ridge Battlegrounds 76
   Memorials in Querciola 76
   German Fortifications on Mount Belvedere 77
   Brazilian War Monument near Gaggio Montano 77

History Museum of Montese 77
Memorials and Models at Castel d'Aiano 78

Chapter 10: Bologna 79
Historical Summary 79
In the Center of Bologna 80
Memorials in Piazza Nettuno 80
Palazzo dell'Archiginnasio 80
Air Raid Signs 81
Jewish Museum 81
Museum of the Resistance 81
On Bologna's Outskirts 82
Memorial Museum of Liberty 82
Bologna War Cemetery *(Commonwealth)* 83
Polish Cemetery 83

Chapter 11 Map 84

Chapter 11: Day Trips from Bologna 85
West of Bologna 85
Deportation Memorial Museum in Carpi 85
Deportation Camp at Fossoli 86
Cervi Museum near Parma 86
Museum of the Partisan Republic, Montefiorino 87
Sites near or in Marzabotto 87
History Park of Monte Sole 87
Memorial Chapel 89
National Etruscan Museum 89
Two Museums 90
"Winter Line" Museum in Livergnano 90
World War II Museum of the Po River, Felonica 91
Ravenna Area 92
Museum of the Battle of the Senio in Alfonsine 92
Villanova Canadian War Cemetery *(Commonwealth)* 92
Italian Military Cemetery at Camerlona 94
Ravenna War Cemetery *(Commonwealth)* 94

Chapter 12: Trieste 95
Historical Summary 95
On the Outskirts of Trieste 96
Civic Museum of the San Sabba Risiera 96
Foiba *(Burial Pit)* Monument at Basovizza 97

In the Center of Trieste 98
    The Great Synagogue 98
    Wagner Museum of the Jewish Community.................................99
    Castle of San Giusto 99

Endnotes..100

Bibliography..101

Selected Films..102

About the Author...103

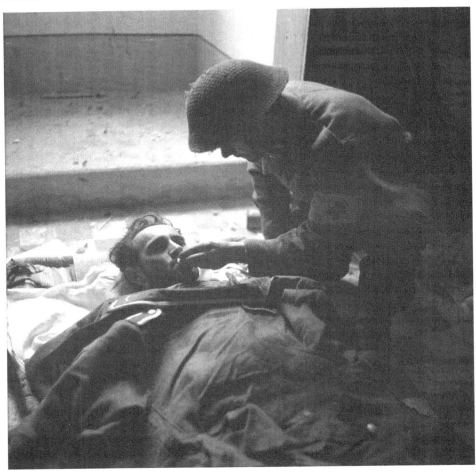

A Canadian medic gives water to a wounded German prisoner in Catona, Italy, December 1943.
Library and Archives Canada

Acknowledgments

I am deeply grateful to these individuals for sharing their knowledge of Italian history and culture with me: Edo Ansaloni, Nadia Baiesi, Joseph Bevilacqua, Michele di Lonardo, Simone Guidorzi, John Luncheon, Umberto and Patrizia Magnani, Elisa Mazzini, Antonio Parisella, Vito Paticchia, Piergiorgio Pieroni, Claudio Silingardi, Stefano Soglia, and Filippo Spadi.

I thank Jerry Spiller, a co-founder of www.articipatory.com, for creating the book's maps. My appreciation goes also to Antonio Parisella, Vito Paticchia, Cindy Blackburn, Jean Saunders-Blanks, Carter Saunders, Barry Coffey, and Jamie Moore for commenting on early versions of this guide, and to Penny Schreiber for editing the final manuscript.

The Department of Classics at the College of Charleston has supported my research over the years. World War II veterans John Duffy, Hugh Evans, John Imbrie, and Eugene Reilly gave me useful tips about memorial sites in Italy. Boyce Blanks was of great help in setting up the book's website, www.travelguidepress.com.

And many thanks to my husband, Richard Saunders, for being the best driver, photographer, and travel companion.

Transportation Tips

Road Maps and Driving in Italy
- This book's maps show the chief roads between the towns and cities noted in chapters 2, 3, 6, 7, 9, and 11. More detailed maps are published by car rental agencies, AAA, Michelin, and Touring Club Italiano.
- In Italy, posted road *signs* normally use arrows and the names of towns to direct drivers. However, *maps* often show a road's official label, which consists of a number and one of these abbreviations: SS (strada statale/state road); SR (strada regionale/regional road); SP (strada provinciale/provincial road). For example, SS64 stands for State Road 64. Those abbreviations are used in this book.
- Roads labeled "E" or "A," such as "A12," are divided expressways with tolls and limited access. Expressway signs usually do show a highway's letter and number.

City Maps
- Hotels and tourist offices in Italy often provide free street maps. Use those to follow the city tours in chapters 4, 5, 7, 10, and 12.
- In Italy, the street number follows the street name, as in this example: Via Tasso 2. That system is used in this book.

Fees, Trains, and the Regions of Italy
- Admission fees are listed only if a site charges a fee; most do not.
- Train schedules are available in English at **www.trenitalia.it**.
- Italy is divided into twenty regions, which are similar in function to provinces in Canada and states in the USA. Examples are Tuscany (Toscana), Umbria, Emilia-Romagna, and Lazio.

Hotels

The author visited the following hotels while researching this book and was not compensated for listing them here.

Chapter 2

Hotel Alba, Via G. Biasi 53, Cassino, tel. 0776121873. www.albahotel.it

Hotel Al Boschetto, Via Ausonia 54, Cassino, tel. 777639131. www.hotelristorantealboschetto.it

Hotel Piazza Marconi, Via Marconi 25, Cassino, tel. 077626025. www.hotelpiazzamarconi.it

Chapter 3

Astura Palace Hotel, Via G. Matteotti 75, Nettuno, tel. 0698056054. www.asturapalace-hotel.it

Chapters 4 and 5

In Rome, hotels near the main train station (called Termini) offer easy access to city buses and the subway. Two good choices in that area are:

Residenza Domiziano, Via San Nicola da Tolentino 50, tel. 0642012998. www.residenzadomiziano.com

Starhotel Metropole, Via Principe Amadeo 3, tel. 064740413. www.starhotels.com

Chapter 6

Relais Montefiore, Piazza della Libertà 8, Montefiore di Conca (near Gemmano and Rimini), tel. 054198029. www.relaismontefiore.it

Hotel Palazzo Viviani, Via Roma 38, Montegridolfo, tel. 0541855350. www.montegridolfo.com

Hotel Alexander, Piazzale Karl Marx 10, Cesena, tel. 054727474. www.albergoalexander.it

Chapter 7

Hotel Enza, Via San Zanobi 45, Florence, tel. 055490990. www.hotelenza.it

Hotel Gallo, Piazza della Repubblica 28, Castel del Rio, tel. 054295924. www.galloegalletto.it

Chapter 8

Rest in Lucca B&B, Via Carlo Angeloni 211, Lucca, tel. 0583312594. www.restinlucca.it

Chapter 9

Hotel Montegrande, Via Marconi 27, Vidiciatico, tel. 053453210.
www.montegrande.it
Hotel Il Fondaccio, Via Gasperini 22, Lizzano in Belvedere, tel. 053451180
Hotel Monte Pizzo, Piazza Montanari 1, Lizzano in Belvedere, tel. 053451055.
www.hotelmontepizzo.it
Hotel Nappini, Via Novembre 3, Lizzano in Belvedere, tel. 051847045.
www.hotelnappini.it
Hotel Miramonti, Via Provinciale 11, Montese, tel. 059981703

Chapter 10

If you are touring Bologna and also taking day trips from there, it is convenient to stay near the central train station. Two good choices in that area are:
Albergo Atlantic, Via Galliera 46, tel. 051248488. www.albergoatlantic.net
Starhotel Excelsior, Viale P. Pietramellara 51, tel. 051246178.
www.starhotels.com

Chapter 11

Please see suggestions for Chapter 10. In addition, a rustic inn called **Il Poggiolo** offers lodgings within the History Park at Via San Martino 25, tel. 0516787100. Book at www.poggiolomontesole.it.

Chapter 12

Grand Hotel Duchi d'Aosta, Piazza dell'Unità 2, Trieste, tel. 0407600011.
www.duchi.eu
James Joyce, Via Cavazzeni 7, Trieste, tel. 040311023.
www.hoteljamesjoyce.com
Urban Hotel Design, Via Androna Chiusa 4, Trieste, tel. 040302065.
www.urbanhotel.it

Introduction: Italy 1914–1945

The Fascist Party comes to power *(1914–1930s)*

At the beginning of the First World War, the government of Italy chose to be neutral. However, lured by promises of territorial gains in Europe and Africa, Italy entered World War I in 1915 on the side of the Allies. By war's end, about 1.7 million Italians had been killed or wounded, and the nation had gained little from its investment of men and material wealth. Thousands of workers had no jobs, and veterans received few rewards for their sacrifices.

As living conditions in postwar Italy worsened, the government struggled to cope with strikes, high unemployment, and other threats to national stability. This fluid environment gave an opening to the Fascist Party, which was founded by Benito Mussolini in 1919. Mussolini and other Fascist leaders drew followers by promising to restore prosperity and stability to the people of Italy. These promises, combined with Mussolini's personal charisma, were effective. The Fascist Party grew rapidly over the next few years, fueled by political unrest and the ruthless tactics of its leaders.

In October 1922, the unrest came to a head when thousands of Fascist Party members converged on Rome to demand that Mussolini be put in charge of the government. Italy's king, Vittorio Emmanuele III, yielded to this pressure by appointing Mussolini prime minister. Mussolini used his office to eliminate opposition to the Fascist Party and to himself. By 1925, he and his associates controlled the government of Italy in a one-party dictatorship. Soon they eliminated the powers of parliament and banned all other political parties. The Fascist Party took over schools and newspapers; it jailed, exiled, or murdered many of its opponents. By the 1930s, the party also controlled significant parts of Italian finance and industry.

As Mussolini became more powerful, he began enlarging Italy's domain through territorial conquest, much in the manner of his heroes, the Roman emperors. Despite the objections of the League of Nations, in 1935 Mussolini sent an army to conquer Ethiopia. This country was an easy target because its soldiers lacked modern weapons and military training.

Mussolini and Hitler cooperate *(1930s)*

While Mussolini was taking charge in Italy, Adolph Hitler was gaining political power in Germany. Hitler became chancellor in 1933 and immediately began establishing his dictatorship. Cooperation between the Italian and German dictators soon followed. Both Mussolini and Hitler sent troops to bolster the Fascist insurgency in Spain's civil war. In 1936, Germany and Italy formed the Rome-Berlin Axis as an expression of their common interests. In 1937, Mussolini announced that Italy would withdraw from the

League of Nations and join Germany and Japan as nonmembers opposed to international cooperation. In 1939, Hitler and Mussolini entered into the Pact of Steel, which outlined common foreign policy objectives for their two nations.

Hitler and Mussolini greet the crowds in Munich, July 1940.
U.S. National Archives

During the 1930s, Mussolini also took steps to align Italian domestic policy with that of Germany. In 1938 Mussolini followed Hitler's lead by instituting laws that segregated Jews from the rest of the nation. Jews were not allowed to teach in state schools and universities, serve in the military, marry Christians, or hire Christian servants. Newspapers were forbidden to employ Jews and even to publish their obituaries.

Germany and Italy declare war *(1939 and 1940)*

On September 1, 1939, Hitler launched the invasion of Poland. Two days later, France and Great Britain declared war against Germany. Mussolini proclaimed Italy's non-belligerency, but then invaded and took control of Albania. When German armies seized Denmark, Norway, Luxembourg, Belgium, the Netherlands, and northern France, Mussolini thought that Germany's victory was certain and that the moment for Italy's alliance with Germany had come.

Hoping to share in the spoils of German conquest, in June 1940 Mussolini declared war on the Allies and dispatched troops to the French Alps. He then tried to seize more territory for the empire that he hoped to build. In August 1940, Italian forces stationed in Ethiopia were ordered to invade Somaliland. In October 1940, Italian troops stationed in Albania were sent to invade Greece. These military operations were not successful. Italian forces not only failed to accomplish their missions but often drew British counterattacks, with the result that Hitler had to send German troops to the rescue.

The United States enters the war *(December 1941)*

The bombing of Pearl Harbor brought the United States into this global conflict. On December 11, 1941, four days after Pearl Harbor, Mussolini joined Hitler in declaring war against the United States. Thus by the end of 1941, Germany and Italy were battling a coalition of nations that would demand unconditional surrender from every member of the Axis alliance.

American and British commanders initially disagreed on how to begin their attack against Germany and its European allies. The American Joint Chiefs of Staff wanted to launch an assault on occupied France from Britain. In contrast, Prime Minister Winston S. Churchill and British military chiefs preferred to begin the attack on Europe from North Africa, where British Commonwealth troops already were battling German and Italian forces. Churchill argued that it would be relatively easy to invade and conquer Italy after taking North Africa.

In 1942, President Franklin D. Roosevelt broke this deadlock by directing his commanders to plan for a campaign in North Africa that year. The invasion of occupied France was postponed to a later date, when there would be more men and supplies. The now-fabled invasion of Normandy finally took place in June 1944.

Armies battle in North Africa and Sicily *(1942–1943)*

In the summer and fall of 1942, the brilliant General Bernard L. Montgomery led British Commonwealth forces against German and Italian armies stationed in North Africa. In late October 1942, Montgomery's troops achieved a decisive victory over Axis forces near the city of El Alamain in northern Egypt. This success showed that Hitler's forces were not invincible and thus marked a turning point in the war.

In November 1942, American and British troops launched an invasion of Morocco and Algeria, which then were controlled by the German-dominated Vichy French government. Some of the Vichy troops fought back, but ultimately they were defeated. Many survivors then joined the Allies in the march toward Tunisia.

In February 1943, Axis troops commanded by Field Marshal Erwin Rommel defeated American forces at the Kasserine Pass in northern Tunisia. General Dwight D. Eisenhower swiftly replaced the American commander with Major General George S. Patton, who was known for his boldness. Patton worked to improve the morale, discipline, and battlefield performance of the troops now under his command. At the same time, the Commonwealth forces commanded by Montgomery continued to win important victories. With these combined efforts, Allied forces controlled the entire coast of North Africa by May 1943.

Political and military leaders agreed that Sicily should be the next objective for Patton's Seventh Army and Montgomery's Eighth Army. On July 10 and 11, 1943, over eighty thousand Allied troops landed along the southern coast of Sicily. They took the island within thirty-nine days, forcing an Axis retreat to mainland Italy.

General George S. Patton confers with a lieutenant near Brolo, Sicily, July 1943.
U.S. National Archives

Mussolini is deposed *(July 1943)*

The victories of the Allies in North Africa and Sicily undermined Mussolini's authority in the eyes of the Italian people, King Vittorio Emmanuele III, and the Fascist Grand Council. On July 19, 1943, Mussolini's reputation as a commander declined further when Allied aircraft bombed the rail yards of Rome, unintentionally killing hundreds of civilians and damaging an ancient basilica. These attacks were the first made against Rome, although Allied bombs had already hit Milan, Turin, and Genoa. The evident strength of the Allied forces encouraged Vittorio Emmanuele and the Fascist Grand Council to topple Mussolini, a move that they had been considering for some time.

On July 24, 1943, the Fascist Grand Council met in central Rome at Palazzo Venezia, a Renaissance palace that housed Mussolini's offices. After hours of discussion, a majority of the council's members voted to remove Mussolini from command of the government and the armed forces. In effect, they fired their dictator. Mussolini, amazed and angered by this vote, then returned to his family's mansion near the center of Rome.

On July 25, Vittorio Emmanuele met with Mussolini at the royal residence in Rome (Villa Savoia, now called Villa Ada) and told him that he must step down. As the dictator left the king's residence, he was met by a police captain and escorted to a waiting ambulance. Guards then took Mussolini to the island of Ponza, not far from Naples. At the end of August he was transferred to the Campo Imperatore Hotel in the rugged mountains several hours east of Rome.

In an evening radio broadcast on July 25, Vittorio Emmanuele announced that he had handed Mussolini's powers over to Marshal Pietro Badoglio, an Italian general. That same evening, Badoglio issued a proclamation that Italy would continue in the war on Germany's side. Many Italians doubted Badoglio's assertion and assumed that the fall of Mussolini meant that the war had ended. Spontaneous celebrations erupted throughout Italy. Even in the Italian prisons where Allied POWs were held, the guards were jubilant. Former British prisoner Eric Newby recalled that his guards threw Mussolini's picture out the window, tore down Fascist posters, and joyfully shouted: "BENITO FINITO."[1]

The overthrow of Mussolini enraged Hitler, who sensed that Italy was close to abandoning its alliance with Germany. Although Hitler decided to play along with the new leaders of Italy, in part to preserve the country as a supply source, he also decided to send in more troops. By the end of August, sixteen German divisions were in Italy, initially split between Rommel and Field Marshal Albert Kesselring. Later that fall, Hitler put Kesselring in charge of all forces in Italy and sent Rommel to prepare for the expected Allied invasion of occupied France.

Italy surrenders *(September 1943)*

Hitler was correct in anticipating that Italy would soon withdraw from its alliance with Germany. In August 1943, Badoglio and Vittorio Emmanuele began secret negotiations for the surrender of Italy to the Allies. On September 3, their representatives signed an unconditional armistice, which General Eisenhower announced through a radio broadcast on September 8. The same evening, Badoglio also spoke on the radio. He reinforced Eisenhower's statement and ordered Italian forces to cease hostilities against the Allies.

A few hours later, Badoglio and Vittorio Emmanuele, perhaps fearing assassination, committed one of the more astonishing acts in Italian history. In the early hours of September 9, they and other Italian leaders deserted Rome for a safe haven with Allied forces in Brindisi, a city on Italy's southeastern coast. In his haste, Badoglio left no one in charge of Rome and abandoned documents that the Nazis used to their advantage when they occupied that city. The abrupt exit of Badoglio, Vittorio Emmanuele, and their colleagues also contributed to the rapid disintegration of the Italian army in the fall of 1943.

German troops occupy Italian towns and cities *(September 1943)*

German leaders had been preparing for Italy's possible defection by flooding that country with thousands of troops, who occupied Italian cities and towns immediately after the armistice. The Germans seized control of local governments, appropriated residences and offices, and took what they pleased in terms of supplies from the civilian population. Italians still loyal to the Fascist cause assisted the occupiers.

Immediately after the armistice, another surprising event occurred. On September 12, German aviators rescued Mussolini from his mountain prison and flew him to Vienna for a reunion with Hitler. Eventually Hitler made Mussolini the head of a puppet regime named the Italian Social Republic. This regime was often called the Salò Republic after the town in northern Italy where it was based.

Italian soldiers and officers took various paths after the armistice. Thousands refused to surrender to the Germans and were executed. The Germans captured six hundred thousand Italian troops and sent them to forced labor sites in Germany or northern Italy, where some deliberately did poor work in order to undercut the German war effort. Many of the soldiers who escaped capture organized paramilitary brigades to fight against the Germans and aid the Allies. However, some joined the German armed forces or served in the army of Mussolini's puppet regime.

Allied forces reach mainland Italy *(September 1943)*

After the conquest of Sicily, the Fifth Army and the Eighth Army were assigned to carry on the campaign against German armies in mainland Italy. The Fifth consisted mainly of American forces, but also contained British units and French colonial troops. The Eighth Army was even more diverse. Made up chiefly of forces from British Commonwealth nations, it had troops from the United Kingdom, India, Canada, New Zealand, South Africa, and Rhodesia. The Eighth Army also included units from Poland, Nepal, Greece, and elsewhere. The exact makeup of each army varied over the course of the Italian campaign.

In September 1943, the Fifth Army and the Eighth Army began their assault on the Italian mainland, which was held by German forces. The Eighth Army made an unopposed crossing from Sicily to the mainland on September 3, 1943. It then advanced north along Italy's eastern coast, seizing the air base at Foggia and the city of Bari. On Italy's western coast, three divisions of the Fifth Army sailed from Sicily and Algeria to the Gulf of Salerno, an area about thirty miles south of Naples. On September 9, 1943, they landed at Salerno and were immediately attacked by the 16th Panzer Division, a unit of the German Tenth Army. The Germans fought so fiercely that they almost pushed the Fifth Army back into the sea. However, after nine days of fighting, the American and British troops compelled the Germans to retreat. The Fifth Army then marched north, reaching Naples at the end of September.

Allied forces advance up the Italian peninsula
(Autumn 1943–Spring 1945)

Prior to the arrival of the Fifth Army, German troops had occupied Naples and were rounding up local men for service in forced labor camps. They also destroyed much of Naples' infrastructure, both to make the city less useful for the approaching Fifth Army and to avenge Italy's defection from its alliance with Germany. They even compelled Neapolitans to participate in demolishing their city.

On September 26, after two weeks of German misrule, several thousand Neapolitans took up arms against the occupiers, using rifles, swords, and whatever makeshift weapons they could find. This revolt continued until September 30, during which time three hundred citizens are said to have died in combat. The film *Four Days of Naples* (1962) vividly depicts the clashes between the occupiers and Neapolitans, whose attacks forced the Germans to leave Naples two days earlier than planned, according to an American intelligence report.[2]

The Fifth Army arrived in Naples shortly after German forces left. Its troops found the city in ruins. The Germans had blown up Naples' source of running water and destroyed over forty sewer lines. They had demolished bridges, generators, substations, telephone lines, and about fifty factories. They had torched the libraries of the Italian Royal Society and the University of Naples, destroying thousands of priceless manuscripts and rare books. They had wrecked Naples' vast port and sunk most ships berthed there. The destruction of the port was not only a loss for Neapolitans but also a handicap for the Allies, who had planned to use it to supply their own troops.

Shortly after their arrival, Fifth Army engineers began reconstructing Naples' port and other basic facilities, while other troops worked to supply Neapolitans with food and water. The Fifth Army then marched north toward the city of Cassino. Bad weather and the rugged terrain conspired to make this advance especially difficult. Legendary American war correspondent Ernie Pyle wrote that "our troops were living in almost inconceivable misery. The fertile black valleys were knee-deep in mud. Thousands of men had not been dry for weeks. Other thousands lay at night in the high mountains with the temperature below freezing and the thin snow drifting over them." The journalist added that the steep terrain aided the enemy: "A mere platoon of Germans, well dug in on a high rock-spined hill, could hold out for a long time against tremendous onslaughts."[3]

While the Fifth Army was advancing toward Cassino, the Eighth Army was working its way up the Adriatic coast. By December 1943, Eighth Army troops had reached the town of Ortona, where they overcame fierce resistance from German forces (see Chapter 6). In January 1944, Fifth Army troops reached Cassino, where strong German defenses prevented an Allied breakthrough until May of 1944 (see Chapter 2). After the liberation of Rome on June 4, 1944, the Fifth Army and the Eighth Army continued to battle their way up the Italian peninsula, regularly assisted by Allied air power (see Chapters 7–12).

In the winter of 1944–45, the two Allied armies entered winter quarters near Bologna. By then it was clear that the Allies would win the war, but each side continued preparing for the spring offensive. In early April 1945, Allied forces began their attack against German troops near Bologna. Although many German soldiers fought back, some abandoned the struggle and surrendered or fled. After the liberation of Bologna on April 21, 1945, the Fifth and Eighth Armies linked up and continued their pursuit of German forces, thousands of whom were taken prisoner.

A small group of Italian partisans dealt quickly with Mussolini. On April 27 they arrested the former dictator with his mistress, Clara Petacci, as the couple attempted to flee to Switzerland. The next day, partisans executed the pair along with other senior Fascist officials, and then hung their bodies upside down in Piazzale Loreto, a public square near Milan's central train station.

During the first week of May, Allied commanders met with their German counterparts to accept the surrender of German forces in Italy.

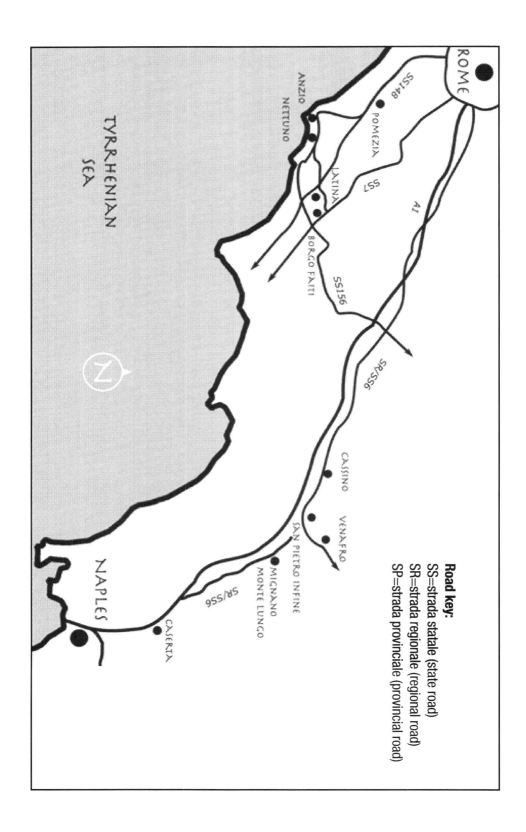

Road key:
SS=strada statale (state road)
SR=strada regionale (regional road)
SP=strada provinciale (provincial road)

Cassino and Caserta

Travel notes: During the first half of 1944, battles and bombings destroyed the city of Cassino, its historic abbey, and nearby villages. Most of these places were rebuilt, some in their original form, but the area's numerous monuments preserve the memory of the war.

Allow two days for seeing the sites described below. If you have three days to spend, also visit the Royal Palace at Caserta, about an hour south of Cassino. That complex, a UNESCO World Heritage site, served as Allied Forces Mediterranean Headquarters from 1943 to 1945.

Trains run frequently between Rome and Cassino. By car, take expressway A1 south from Rome and exit at Cassino; follow signs to the city center (*centro*).

Historical summary: Over the centuries, Cassino and its neighbors have often suffered the effects of war. This area became a battleground again toward the end of 1943, when German troops withdrew from southern Italy to Cassino. The city had been fortified prior to late 1943 because it stood on a major road to Rome and also was part of the Gustav Line, the most elaborate German defensive system south of Rome. This "line" was a series of bunkers, turrets, gun emplacements, barbed wire, land mines, and other defenses installed across Italy, from the western coast to a point near Ortona on the Adriatic. The Gustav Line was intended to help the Germans prevent or at least slow the Allied advance up the peninsula.

German commanders instructed their troops to hold Cassino and its surrounding mountains at all costs. Allied commanders were equally determined that their forces would break through at Cassino and advance north toward Rome and beyond. Thousands of soldiers struggled and died to achieve those goals, as the area war cemeteries attest.

In January 1944, selected Fifth Army troops attempted to advance by crossing the Rapido River at the village of Sant'Angelo in Theodice, just south of Cassino. Although the soldiers made heroic efforts to accomplish their objective, German troops held the hills above the river and thus had an easy shot at the men attempting to cross. Many men drowned in the river or were killed by land mines. Some soldiers and officers attributed the high casualty rate to poor planning by the Fifth Army commander, Lieutenant General Mark W. Clark.[4]

In February, some Allied commanders proposed a second strategy for breaking through the Gustav Line. Claiming that the abbey was sheltering German troops (probably not the case), they argued that it had to be destroyed before more Allied troops were committed to the field. This plan generated much debate, since the abbey was a sacred place and an artistic treasure, but ultimately the plan was followed. On February 15, 1944, Allied bombers dropped tons of explosives on the abbey, reducing it to rubble and killing hundreds of civilians who had taken refuge within its walls. Allied forces then tried to capture the site but failed to do so, in part because the destruction of the abbey had actually bolstered the

Germans' advantage. With the monks gone, German troops could position themselves in the abbey's ruins, a good place to observe Allied troop movements.

As part of their third attempt to break through German defenses, Allied commanders ordered the destruction of Cassino itself. On March 15, over four hundred bombers dropped one thousand tons of bombs on the city, turning it into fiery rubble. Allied forces then battled German troops within its ruins and in the surrounding mountains for almost two weeks. However, at the end of March the Germans still controlled much of the area where the city and the abbey had stood, and thus could continue to prevent an Allied breakthrough.

In mid-April, Allied commanders finally devised a plan that enabled their armies to advance north. After ordering their troops to cease hostilities along the Gustav Line for several weeks, they then secretly brought most of the Eighth Army from the Adriatic coast to Cassino. This move was undertaken when several high-ranking German officers were absent. On May 11, 1944, Allied troops launched a massive new attack against German forces at Cassino. This hard-fought operation cost many lives, but ultimately did succeed. By May 18, the Germans had retreated from Cassino and were heading north toward their next defensive line, while the Allies were advancing to Rome and other points north.

An Italian soldier who passed through Cassino in the summer of 1944 described the ruins of the city thus: "Not only had all the buildings been reduced to debris but also every living creature, vegetation too, had been killed. Motionless water stagnated on the enclosed flat land between the mountains where the city once rose and flooded the large expanse of ruins; there wasn't a single tree or shrub as far as the eye could see."[5]

SITES WITHIN CASSINO
Abbey of Monte Cassino *(Abbazia di Monte Cassino)*
Tel. 0776311529; www.montecassino.it

Hours: Daily 8:30am–12:30pm and 3:30pm–5pm (summer months until 6pm).

Directions: This imposing complex stands on a mountain overlooking the town. By car, take the paved road that runs uphill from town to the abbey's parking lot. Or, take the public bus that runs between the train station and abbey several times per day. Check the bus schedule on the abbey website or at the train station.

What to see: The current abbey is a replica of the structure destroyed by bombs on February 15, 1944. Rebuilt soon after the war, this beautiful place now welcomes visitors and occasionally hosts retreats.

Saint Benedict, the patron saint of Europe, founded the Benedictine order here in the early sixth century CE. Marauders destroyed the original abbey in 577. It was rebuilt, but raiders destroyed it a second time in 883. The faithful then reconstructed the abbey. However, in 1349 an earthquake leveled it for a third time. After the earthquake, the abbey was rebuilt and later enlarged. The Italian government declared it a national monument in 1866. The fourth reconstruction took place after the abbey was bombed in February 1944.

From the abbey's parking lot and bus stop, a walkway leads to massive entrance doors.

Immediately within the entrance, a shop sells postcards, paintings, and guidebooks in English and other languages. Three cloisters stand just outside the shop. The first, called the Entrance Cloister, has a statue group that represents the dying Saint Benedict supported by two monks. The second is the Bramante Cloister, named after the famous Renaissance architect. From its balcony you can see the Liri Valley and the roads to Rome that Allied soldiers fought so hard to reach. Visible also is the hillside Polish cemetery, which has over one thousand graves.

The third cloister, the Benefactors, is named after the popes and kings who contributed to the building and maintenance of the abbey. From these cloisters, a staircase leads visitors up to the basilica's entrance. Its massive bronze doors depict events in Saint Benedict's life and the four destructions of the abbey.

The interior of the basilica is as grand as its exterior. Frescoes adorn its walls and ceilings. Elaborately carved choir stalls stand behind the central altar. Lustrous mosaics decorate the crypt, which can be reached by a staircase to the side of the central altar. Underneath the altar lie the remains of Saint Benedict and his sister, Saint Scholastica.

The abbey also has a small museum that holds ancient manuscripts, sculptures and paintings. Its hours are those of the abbey except in winter, when it is open only on Sundays.

The ruins of the Abbey of Monte Cassino after the bombing in February 1944.
Frank J. Davis Collection, Southern Methodist University

Polish Cemetery *(Cimitero Polacco)*

Hours: *May 16–September 30*, daily 9am–11:45am and 3pm–5:45pm; *October 1–May 15*, daily 9am–11:45am and 2pm–4:45pm.

Directions: This mountainside cemetery is just off the road that runs between Cassino and the abbey. Parking is available.

What to see: 1,052 burials. Polish units fought alongside British Commonwealth troops in the Eighth Army during the Italian campaign. A large cross and a stone monument honor these soldiers, whose commander, General Wladyslaw Anders (1892–1970), also is buried here. In 1949 Anders published *An Army in Exile*, a book about his wartime experiences.

Historiale

Via San Marco 23, tel. 0776313852; www.historiale.it

Hours: *April 1–September 30,* daily except Saturday, 10am–6pm.

Admission: €10 adults; €6 children

Directions/what to see: From the abbey, return to the Cassino train station. From there, walk left on Via Bonomi for two blocks to Via San Marco. Turn left and follow signs to the complex, which includes a multimedia museum, bookstore, cafeteria, and parking area. The museum concentrates on local battles and the wartime sufferings of area civilians. Its special effects were designed by Carlo Rambaldi, a three-time Oscar winner. Presentations are in Italian and English.

Cassino War Cemetery *(Commonwealth)*

Via Sant'Angelo; www.cwgc.org/admin/files/Italy.pdf

Hours: *Summer*, daily 7am–12pm and 1pm–2:30pm; *winter* open at 8am.

Directions: From Historiale (described above), return to Via Bonomi and turn left. Walk several blocks down that street to Via Sant'Angelo. There turn left and take the bridge over the train tracks. Continue a few hundred yards more to the parking lot in front of the cemetery, which is less than a mile from Historiale.

What to see: 4,271 burials. Cassino is the largest of the thirty-seven Second World War Commonwealth cemeteries in Italy. A small building within the well-maintained grounds contains a register of the graves. Most headstones are inscribed with a soldier's name, unit, date of death, and age at time of death; at the top is carved the unit crest. Some stones also have a few lines of prose or verse chosen by the individual's family or friends. The markers for those who could not be identified note the grave of a soldier "known unto God." Large marble slabs bear the names of 4,153 soldiers missing in action.

About a mile farther down Via Sant'Angelo on the left stands a monument honoring soldiers of the Bedfordshire and Hertfordshire Regiment who fought at Cassino and elsewhere in Italy.

Memorials in the Center of Cassino

Hours: Best seen in daylight.

Directions/what to see: Several war memorials stand in Piazza Gasperi, a large square seven blocks north of the train station. This piazza has several small parks, one of which contains World War II artillery and tanks. To the left of tanks is a *sasso votivo* (votive stone) dedicated to citizens who died in the bombing of Cassino or in the struggle to liberate Italy from the Germans.

Two blocks east of Piazza Gasperi is Piazza XV Febbraio (February 15, the date that the abbey was bombed). In this piazza stands a stone memorial that describes the abbey's destruction; it also notes the abbot's request that it be rebuilt "*dove era, come era*" (where it was, as it was). This monument is part of a project called "The Memory of Stone," which has installed war memorials throughout the city.

SITES NEAR CASSINO

Complete descriptions and driving directions are given below. If you prefer to hire a professional guide who also can provide transportation, contact Mr. Michele Di Lonardo (fluent in English, German, French, Italian) at *micheledilonardo@hotmail.com*.

History Memorial Park *(Parco della Memoria Storica)* of San Pietro Infine

Piazza San Nicola, tel. 3331381559; www.parcodellamemoriastorica.com

Hours: The park is open in daylight; the exhibit building by appointment.

Directions: From Cassino, take SS6 for about seven miles southeast to the village of San Pietro Infine and follow signs uphill to the park, which contains the remains of the original village.

What to see: Allied and German troops battled in and around San Pietro Infine for nine days in December 1943. By the end of that time period, the Allies had forced the Germans to retreat, thus achieving their goal of securing the advance toward Cassino. However, San Pietro Infine was reduced to rubble.

After the war, a new village was rebuilt nearby and given the same name. The hilltop ruins of the original village were turned into a park that powerfully conveys war's ability to destroy. Acres of bombed stone buildings remain, most without roofs and often missing walls. Although vegetation covers much of the area, it is still possible to walk on some of the narrow streets and imagine how the buildings looked before the war. The park also includes the caves where hundreds of civilians hid during bombardments.

At the park's entrance stands an exhibit building designed and equipped by Carlo Rambaldi, who has won three Academy Awards for special effects. One room of that building shows a forty-minute film drawn from John Huston's wartime documentary, *The Battle of San Pietro*. This film vividly depicts the realities of war.

Canadian officer searches a German POW, 1944.
Library and Archives Canada

Italian Military Cemetery *(Sacrario Militare Italiano)* at Mignano Monte Lungo

www.prolocomignano.it

Hours: *May 16–September 30*, daily 8:30am–1pm and 1:30–5.15pm.
Other months, closings at 3:45pm.

Directions: By car from San Pietro Infine (described above), continue on SS6 south for two miles. The cemetery lies just off SS6 on a hillside outside the village of Mignano Monte Lungo and is marked by a prominent stone sign.

What to see: 975 burials. On December 8, 1943, Italian forces battled German troops on this very site. The Italians suffered many casualties, but with a new plan of attack overcame the Germans by December 16. Commemorative ceremonies are held here every December.

This cemetery consists of seven terraces crowned by a marble chapel that contains an altar with a sculpture of a soldier and Christ. The Latin inscription over the altar reads: "mortui ut patria vivat" (they died so that their country might live). The forty-eight men killed in battle here rest in the chapel's wall niches. The terraces hold over nine hundred graves of Italians who fought elsewhere to free their country from the Germans.

Across the road from the cemetery stands a small museum that displays weapons and photographs. At the top of the hill above the cemetery, a large terrace provides views of the former battlegrounds. In its center stands a memorial pillar topped with a statue.

French War Cemetery *(Cimitero Militare Francese)* in Venafro

Hours: Monday–Friday 7am–4pm; weekends 9am–1pm.

Directions: From San Pietro Infine, take SS6 DIR east for eight miles to the town of Venafro, where signs indicate the road to the cemetery (*cimitero)* on its outskirts. Venafro also is a short drive from Cassino.

What to see: 4,922 burials. This site has graves of soldiers from France and its colonies. Most headstones are inscribed with a man's name, rank, and date of death. All grave markers also have the motto, "Mort pour la France" (died for France). A white stucco minaret and a chapel topped by a cross indicate that both Christian and Muslim soldiers are buried here.

German Military Cemetery *(Deutscher Soldatenfriedhof)* at Caira

Hours: *Summer,* daily 8am–6pm; *winter,* daily 9am–4pm.

Directions/what to see: 20,000 burials. From Cassino, drive north for two miles on Via Sferracavalli toward the village of Caira and turn at the sign for the cemetery. Each headstone marks the grave of several people and lists their names along with dates of birth and death. The grounds are well-maintained and adorned with tall cypress trees.

36th Division Monument and Peace Bell Tower

Hours: Best seen in daylight.

Directions/what to see: From Cassino, drive south on Via Sant'Angelo for four miles to the village of Sant'Angelo in Theodice. In its central piazza stands a monument to the U.S. 36th Division, which lost many men here in a disastrous attack in mid-January 1944. Next to the piazza is a bridge; across the bridge stands a bell tower erected by a local group, Associazione Campana della Pace (Peace Bell Association). The tower stands near the spot where U.S. 36th Division troops crossed. Its bells ring daily to honor soldiers who fought at Cassino.

Cassino War Memorial

www.montecassino1944.it

This exhibit has closed but will reopen in another location. The website has links to information in English.

CASERTA

Royal Palace of Caserta *(Reggia di Caserta)*

Via Douhet 22; www.reggiadicaserta.beniculturali.it (click on "Guida Multilingue" for an English version)

Hours: The palace and gardens open at 8:30am, Wednesday–Sunday. The palace closes at 7:30pm; the gardens at various times: *June–August*, 6pm; *May and September,* 5:30pm; *April*, 5pm; *October*, 4:30pm; *March*, 4pm; *November–February*, 2:30pm.

Admission: €9 for the palace and gardens; less for partial tickets

Directions: By car, take expressway A1 and exit at Caserta Nord (North); follow signs for the palace and parking (*parcheggio comunale*). By train, Caserta is about an hour south of Cassino. The palace is a five-minute walk from the station.

What to see: This lavish structure of twelve hundred rooms was built in the eighteenth century and is a UNESCO World Heritage site. Visitors may tour the elaborate royal apartments and the lush formal gardens.

The Fifth Army began using this property in late 1943. From July 1944 until the final days of the war, it served as Allied Forces Mediterranean Headquarters. Soldiers on leave came here for rest and relaxation; a military hospital cared for the injured. At the end of the war, German officials met here with Allied leaders to sign documents confirming the unconditional surrender of German forces in Italy.

Caserta War Cemetery *(Commonwealth)*

Via Sant'Angelo; www.cwgc.org/admin/files/Italy.pdf

Hours: Open daily during daylight.

Directions: Ask at the Royal Palace (described above) for directions to this cemetery. Or, if coming from Rome, take expressway A1 and exit at Caserta Nord (North). Turn left at the first set of traffic lights and continue along that road for about a mile. Just before an army barracks, turn left down a small road. At the three-way junction, turn right and drive under a bridge to a crossroads, where a sign for the cemetery appears. Follow that sign to the cemetery, which adjoins a larger municipal graveyard.

What to see: 755 burials. A plaque notes that some of those buried here died in the military hospital at the Royal Palace, while others were killed in combat at the nearby Volturno

River. Most grave markers are inscribed with a soldier's name, unit, date of death, and age at time of death; the unit crest is carved at the top. Some stones also have a few lines of prose or verse chosen by the individual's family or friends. The graves of those who could not be identified note the burial of a soldier "known unto God."

An American medic treats a wounded soldier in Italy, 1943.
U.S. National Archives

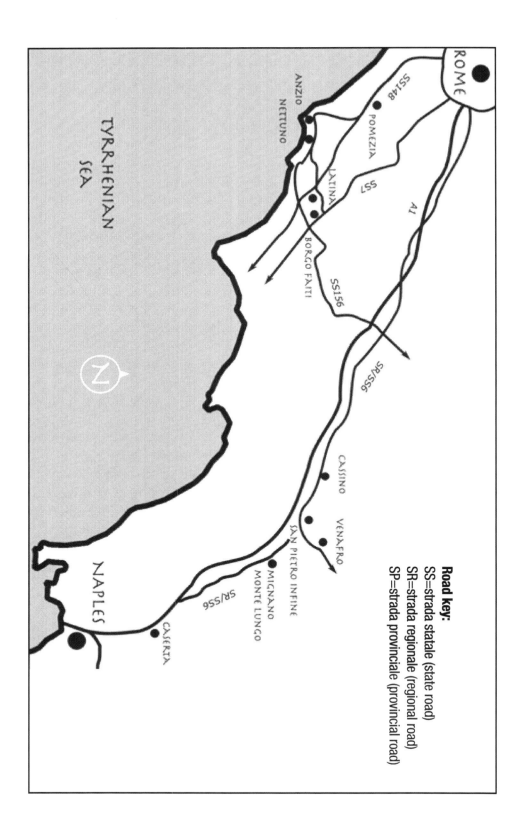

ROME

ANZIO
NETTUNO

TYRRHENIAN
SEA

POMEZIA

SS148

SS7

LATINA

A1

BORGO FAITI

SS156

SR/SS6

N

CASSINO

VENAFRO

SAN PIETRO INFINE

MIGNANO

MONTE LUNGO

SR/SS6

NAPLES

CASERTA

Road Key:
SS=strada statale (state road)
SR=strada regionale (regional road)
SP=strada provinciale (provincial road)

Pomezia, Anzio, Nettuno, and Borgo Faiti

Travel notes: Anzio and Nettuno are adjoining beach communities about thirty miles south of Rome. During the first half of 1944, over two hundred thousand Allied and German soldiers battled in this area. To tour Anzio and Nettuno in one day, arrive early in the morning. If you drive from Rome to Anzio, the German cemetery near the town of Pomezia can be visited on the way.

People with two days to spend can use the second day to visit a large World War II museum near the village of Borgo Faiti.

General tourist information in English: www.laziocoast.it/en/en

Historical summary: In early 1944, Allied commanders sent one hundred thousand troops to the beaches of Anzio and Nettuno. The chief purpose of this operation was to draw German forces away from Cassino, where they were blocking the Allied advance toward Rome and northern Italy.

Tens of thousands of Allied troops were involved in weeks of preparation and practice for this assault. They boarded ship near Naples during the third week of January and began disembarking at Anzio and Nettuno in the early hours of January 22, 1944. The initial landings went smoothly, in part because the Germans had expected the Allies to come ashore elsewhere and so had left those towns minimally defended. The first men on shore met little resistance and were able to push the beachhead three miles inland. By midnight, thirty-six thousand Allied troops had disembarked. By the end of January, about sixty-one thousand troops had landed. By February that number grew to one hundred thousand.

The German commanders quickly learned about the Allied landings and acted promptly. By January 30, they had about seventy thousand troops in the area. More German troops arrived in February, bringing their total to over one hundred thousand. In addition, German bombers began sinking Allied ships in the waters near Anzio.

Although the Germans were not able to push the Allies back into the sea, as Hitler had demanded, they did succeed in trapping Allied troops in the beachhead until May 1944. Wet weather and the area's flat terrain contributed to the difficulty of combat at Anzio and Nettuno. In the winter and spring of 1944, heavy rains soaked the ground, making it too muddy for tanks to move with ease. Allied troops had to attack by advancing over open fields, which offered little cover and made men easy targets for German field artillery and aerial bombings. Even those serving far behind the front lines were injured or killed. The American war correspondent Ernie Pyle observed that people "whose jobs through all the wars of history have been safe ones were as vulnerable as the fighting man. Bakers and typewriter repairmen and clerks were not immune from shells and bombs. Table waiters were in the same boat."[6]

In mid-May, the Allies finally mounted an offensive strong enough to penetrate German defenses. By May 24, German resistance was fading and Allied soldiers had killed or captured hundreds of enemy combatants. Once Allied forces had broken through the German lines, the Eighth Army pursued the Germans north, while the Fifth Army advanced to Rome. The German soldiers holding Rome withdrew just before the Fifth Army's arrival in early June. Contemporary photographs show joyful Romans embracing Allied soldiers. Although the Fifth Army's time in Rome was brief, American veteran Warren Taney remembered that "people were glad to see us. They lined the streets for miles, waving and cheering us. They were kissing each other, some throwing flowers at us. We were all amazed at the beautiful buildings and girls."[7]

POMEZIA
German Military Cemetery *(Deutscher Soldatenfriedhof)*

Hours: Open daily at 8am, with various closings: *April–September* 7pm; *March and October* 6pm; *November* 5pm; *December–February* 4pm.

Directions/what to see: 27,423 burials. This site lies about twenty miles south of Rome and just off SS148, the road to Anzio. It shares a fence with an adjacent municipal cemetery. From Rome, take SS148, exit right at the sign for *cimitero*, and turn into the small parking lot. Walk uphill to a brick entrance building and tree-lined grounds. Each headstone marks the grave of up to six people. Their names, along with dates of birth and death, appear on the front and back of the markers. At one end of the lawn stands a statue group whose inscription says: "Unser Friede Liegt in Seinem Willen" (Our peace lies in His will).

ANZIO
Beachhead Museum *(Museo dello Sbarco di Anzio)*
Via di Villa Adele, tel. 069848059; www.sbarcodianzio.it

Hours: *September–June*, Tuesday/Thursday–Sunday, 10:30am–12:30pm and 4pm–6pm. *July and August*, same days, 10:30am–12:30pm and 5pm–7pm.

Directions: By train from Rome, exit at the Anzio stop (**not** "Anzio Colonna"). As you leave the station, turn left and walk a few hundred yards down Via Menacacci to Via degli Elci. Turn right and walk two blocks to the museum, which is in a mansion called Villa Adele. The villa also hosts an impressive collection of ancient sculpture and art.

By car from Rome, take SS148 to the Anzio exit, follow signs to the train station, and then use the directions in the above paragraph.

What to see: The Beachhead Museum displays weapons, equipment, uniforms, photographs of the landings, and German propaganda posters. The latter were designed to impress Italians with Germany's power. One poster shows gigantic German cannons and airplanes destroying tiny Allied forces. A second depicts a smiling German soldier stretching out his hand; written on the poster is the sentence: "La Germania è veramente vostro amico" (Germany is truly your friend). A third poster portrays an Italian civilian being shot by German soldiers as a warning to anyone who would betray the Fascist-Nazi cause.

Soldiers of the First Special Service Force in a mortar pit at Anzio, April 1944.
Library and Archives Canada

In the museum's front garden stands a monument to officers and soldiers of the Sherwood Foresters 2nd Battalion who died at Anzio.

Anzio War Cemeteries *(Commonwealth)*

On SS207, also known as Via Nettunense
www.cwgc.org/admin/files/Italy.pdf

Hours: Open daily during daylight.

Directions/what to see: If you do not have a car, take a cab from the Anzio train station to the cemeteries. The smaller Anzio cemetery (1,056 burials) lies about a mile from the station and adjoins the municipal graveyard. Its hillside setting furnishes a spectacular view of the sea.

The larger Beach Head Cemetery (2,315 burials) is about two miles farther north on SS207. In both locations, plaques summarize the Italian campaign in English. A soldier's name and unit are inscribed on most headstones. Some markers also have a few sentences chosen by the individual's friends or family. For example, on one is engraved: "Not in his native land but beneath foreign skies/far from those who love him in a hero's grave he lies." On another is written: "He went to do his bit for king and country and we shall never forget him."

Memorials at the Anzio Harbor

Hours: Best seen in daylight.

Directions/what to see: The walk from the museum or Anzio train station to the harbor is less than a mile. Go down Viale Claudio Paolini and through Piazza Battista to Via Mimma Pollastrini. There turn left and walk a block to the waterfront, where a tall dark-gray obelisk honors those who died at Anzio. The obelisk overlooks the harbor, which was filled with Allied ships during the landings. Today, tourist and commuter boats depart from here to Ponza and other islands visible in the distance.

From the obelisk, walk along the waterfront boulevard (Via Porto Innocenziano) to building #13, where a plaque honors the U.S. 488th Port Battalion. Continue on to building #40, whose façade displays plaques that honor three British units: the 1st Battalion of the Duke of Wellington's Regiment, the 1st Battalion King's Shropshire Light Infantry, and the shipmates of the HMS Spartan, a British ship sunk by German action in January 1944. One block from the waterfront is Piazza Pia, Anzio's attractive central square.

NETTUNO

Nettuno (Neptune) is a cheerful town that centers on its seaside boulevard, Via Matteotti. That street is lined with hotels, restaurants, and ice cream parlors, and has a pleasant walkway that overlooks Nettuno's beaches. At Via Matteotti's northern end stands the town's charming medieval quarter, which welcomes visitors and shelters several restaurants within its massive stone walls.

Sicily-Rome American Cemetery and Memorial

Nettuno, tel. 069880284; www.abmc.gov/cemeteries/cemeteries/sr.php

Hours: Daily 8am–4:30pm; closed December 25 and January 1.

Directions: By car from Rome, take SS148 and exit at Campoverde/Nettuno. Follow signs to the cemetery, which is about six miles from the exit and overlooks Piazzale John Kennedy. A superstore called "PAM" stands nearby.

By train from Anzio or Rome, exit at the Nettuno station, turn right on the street (Via Cavour) that parallels the tracks, and walk two blocks to Via Santa Maria. There turn right (a sign points the way) and continue for six blocks to the well-marked cemetery entrance.

What to see: This beautifully-maintained cemetery covers seventy-seven acres and has almost eight thousand graves. Most of the soldiers buried here died in Sicily, southern Italy, or at the Anzio-Nettuno beachhead. The majority of headstones bear an individual's name, rank, native state, and date of death. For those whose bodies could not be identified, the headstones note: "Here rests in honored glory a comrade in arms known but to God."

At the far end stands a memorial chapel whose walls are inscribed with the names of soldiers missing in action. Near the chapel, huge battle maps with English texts explain the Italian campaign. Veterans, civilians, and soldiers gather here to pay tribute with speeches and hymns on the United States' Memorial Day, the last Monday in May.

In the reception building, which once was the site of a field hospital, visitors can watch a short film, obtain maps, and speak with the superintendent. To see a particular grave, ask the superintendent about the books and online sources that show where each person is buried. The graves are not arranged alphabetically.

Plans have been approved for the construction of a new library and learning center next to the reception building. This center will provide information about other World War II monuments in the area. It also will highlight local battles and use interactive media to present the history of the Italian campaign and individual war stories. Among the sites that will be featured is the nearby village of Cisterna, which American soldiers tried to capture in January 1944. Cisterna was of strategic importance because it stood on the road from Anzio to Rome. Allied intelligence reported that it was being held by only a small number of Germans. The troops assigned to capture Cisterna included three battalions of U.S. Rangers. However, *eleven* German battalions were defending Cisterna, a number three times greater than intelligence had reported. The results were disastrous for the U.S. Rangers. The 1st and 3rd battalions lost all but eight of their 767 men, with three hundred soldiers killed and the rest taken prisoner. The 4th battalion endured 50 percent casualties.[8]

Monuments in the Center of Nettuno

Hours: Best seen in daylight.

Directions/what to see: From the American cemetery, walk back to the harbor on Via Santa Maria. Turn left on Via Matteotti and walk one block to Piazza Battisti, which contains a war memorial, a statue of a woman on a stone base. The inscription on the base reads: "Nettuno ai suoi figli caduti per la patria" (Nettuno to its sons who died for the fatherland).

To the left of the statue is a second memorial donated by the U.S. 34th Division. Its inscription praises Americans and Italians who "joined together to bring freedom" to Italy and adds this thought: "Let the sacrifice of the soldiers and civilians who died in World War II never be forgotten."

From the piazza, walk a block north to Via Matteotti #20. Over the door of that building, a plaque notes that the Allied Military Government (AMG) occupied space here after the January 1944 landing.

Across the street, a plaque near the façade of a coffee house (Caffè Volpi) honors the local rebellion against Nazis and Fascists on September 8, 1943, the day that the armistice between Italy and the Allies was announced.

Museum of the Allied Landing *(Museo dello Sbarco Alleato)*
Via Gramsci 5 (a continuation of Via Matteotti), tel. 069803620

Hours: Tuesday–Friday 9:15am–1:30pm; Tuesdays/Thursdays also 3:30pm–5:30pm.

Directions/what to see: This museum is set in a sixteenth-century fort called Forte Sangallo, two blocks north of Nettuno's medieval quarter. Its chief attraction is a display of 250 photos taken in this area between January and May 1944. The photos show such activities and objects as: Allied soldiers unloading tanks from ships; technicians removing mines from the beaches; troops hunkered down in trenches; bombed waterfront buildings in Anzio and Nettuno; subterranean military headquarters; and Anzio Annie, the immense mobile cannon used by the Germans. This museum also displays World War II uniforms, helmets, weapons, and other military equipment.

Borgo Faiti
History Museum *(Museo Storico, La Piana delle Orme)*
Via Migiliara 43.5, tel. 0773258708; www.pianadelleorme.it (click on British flag for English version)

Hours: *April–October*, Monday–Friday 9am–8pm, weekends 9am–7pm; *November–March*, Monday–Friday 9am–6pm, weekends 9am–7pm.

Admission: €12 adults; €8 children

Directions: Allow two or three hours to visit this large museum, which is best reached by car. From Nettuno, take Via Acciarella east. That road becomes SP106B, also known as Strada Foligno. Continue east, following signs for Latina, Borgo Faiti, and the museum.

If you are driving from Rome, take SS148 south. Exit at the sign for Pomezia/Latina and follow signs for Borgo Faiti and the museum, which stands in the middle of cultivated fields. Alternatively, take a train from Rome to Latina and then a cab to the museum. The round-trip cab fare will be at least €50.

What to see: This museum has ten large buildings and several outdoor exhibits. In four of the buildings, life-size model soldiers stand in settings that represent World War II battles in North Africa, Sicily, Cassino, Anzio, and Nettuno. Audio and visual effects enliven these displays. Posters in English, German, and Italian provide details about individual battles and the general aims of the war.

Other exhibit halls contain vintage military vehicles, early twentieth-century farm machines, and antique toys. Another building features a display about the Pontine Marshes, which lay between Rome and Naples. That area was unsuitable for farming until a reclamation project initiated by Mussolini turned the marshes into arable land. Photographs in the museum show Mussolini inspecting the progress of this project.

Rome *(Part A)*

Travel notes: This chapter's tour takes a full day. It begins at a basilica bombed in 1943 and ends at Rome's Jewish Museum. Public buses and the subway provide quick transportation to all sites. Obtain a free street map from your hotel and use the directions given below.

If you are planning to visit many additional sites in Rome, consider buying a copy of *Roma Metro-Bus Map*, which shows all streets and bus routes in Rome. This inexpensive map is sold at train stations, bookstores, and tourist shops.

General tourist information in English: http://en.turismoroma.it

Historical summary: On July 19, 1943, in an effort to hinder German transport capabilities, the Allies bombed Rome's central rail yards. Those yards were (and still are) close to the Basilica of San Lorenzo and Rome's largest municipal cemetery, both of which were damaged, although they were not targets. Tragically, these bombings also killed hundreds of civilians and injured thousands more in the surrounding neighborhood. This attack stunned the people of Rome, who up to this point had been spared aerial assaults. It likewise shocked Pope Pius XII, who came to the bombed basilica that afternoon. There he addressed a welcoming crowd of survivors.

The assault on Rome and other events encouraged the Fascist Grand Council and King Vittorio Emmanuele III to depose Mussolini, a move they had been considering for some time. The council and king forced Mussolini from power on July 25, a week after the Allies bombed Rome.

About seven weeks after Mussolini was deposed, Italy withdrew from its alliance with Germany and surrendered to the Allies. German leaders had been preparing for Italy's possible defection by sending large numbers of troops into the country. As a result, German forces were able to occupy many Italian towns and cities almost immediately after the armistice.

In some locations, citizens confronted the occupiers. For example, on September 10 in Rome, thousands of Italian civilians and soldiers tried to keep German troops from entering the city at Porta San Paolo and other major entry points. However, within two days the well-armed German forces suppressed this initial resistance. They settled in Rome's historic center, took control of local government, and placed tight controls on civilian activity.

In late September 1943, Nazi leaders ordered the Gestapo chief in Rome to make plans for deporting Roman Jews to concentration camps in Poland or Austria. Within a month, German troops were rounding up Jews in Rome's ghetto. On October 18, the Germans placed over one thousand Jews in freight cars and sent them to Auschwitz, a concentration camp in Poland, where most died. More details of this terrible story are given below.

SITES

Basilica of Saint Lawrence outside the walls
(Basilica di San Lorenzo fuori le mura)

Piazzale Verano

Hours: Daily 8am–noon and 3pm–6pm.

Directions: The basilica is nine blocks north of Rome's chief train station (Termini). Take bus #492 from its stop on Via Volturno, which is one block from the train station. Exit at Piazzale Verano, the large square in front of the basilica. San Lorenzo's grounds border the stone walls of the municipal cemetery, called Campo Verano.

Alternatively, take the subway to the Policlinico stop and walk two long blocks down Viale Regina Elena to the basilica. This route passes by university and hospital buildings.

What to see: Allied bombers accidentally damaged San Lorenzo in 1943. It was restored soon after the war. Both the interior and exterior of this basilica possess an austere majesty appropriate to the sad events that occurred here. War monuments mingle with far older works dedicated to Roman Catholic saints.

The basilica's portico has several memorials. A plaque to the right of the central doors thanks Pope Pius XII for his efforts to preserve Rome during the war. On the left side of the portico rests the tomb of a major figure in modern Italy, Alcide De Gasperi (1881-1954). During the war, De Gasperi helped create a political party, the Christian Democrats, and served as prime minister of Italy from 1945 to 1953. The stone plaque on his tomb is inscribed with a Latin sentence that means: "May the light of eternal rest shine on one who loved peace and his country."

Circling the top of the portico are dozens of frescoes depicting events in the lives of San Lorenzo and San Stefano, early Christian martyrs. According to tradition, San Lorenzo was executed on this spot about 258 CE. In the fourth century, Emperor Constantine built a basilica where San Lorenzo is said to have died. Between 579 and 590, Pope Pelagius II constructed a new basilica on the same location. Other popes added to the sixth-century structure.

The tombs of San Lorenzo and some early popes rest in the crypt. On the basilica's right aisle is a door to a hall that leads to the sacristy (*sacrestia*) and cloister (*chiostro*). The cloister contains a piece of a bomb that fell on San Lorenzo, as well as many ancient building fragments. A Latin inscription next to the bomb fragment makes this prayer: "Give us peace in our time."

The large mosaic in the basilica's central aisle replaces what was destroyed by a bomb. The mosaic's Latin inscription notes that the basilica was ravaged by war (*bello*) on July 19, 1943, and restored with God's help (*deo adiuvante*).

A large statue of Pope Pius XII stands in a grassy area near the basilica. The Italian inscription on its base notes that he "here aided the bombed city with the comfort of faith" by visiting the site immediately after the bomb attack. Hours after the pope's visit, the king of Italy came to San Lorenzo and received a hostile reception. People reportedly threw stones and shouted that they wanted peace, not charity, as the king's aide began handing out money.[9] Mussolini also visited the basilica that same night and met an angry reception from residents who had lost relatives in the bombing. Many locals viewed the attack on Rome as further proof of Mussolini's incompetence.

St. Paul's Gate *(Porta San Paolo)*

Hours: This site in a southern section of Rome is best visited in daylight.

Directions: From San Lorenzo, take tram #3 southbound for about three miles to Porta San Paolo, a historic city gate. That tram passes by the Colosseum and other famous buildings.

From other parts of the city, take the subway to the Piramide (Pyramid) stop. Porta San Paolo stands next to an eighty-foot pyramid built by a Roman official in 12 CE as his future tomb.

What to see: At this ancient gate, local citizens and Italian soldiers tried to keep the German troops from entering the city on September 10, 1943. Women, men, and boys fired from the surrounding rooftops and clashed with German soldiers in the streets. The fighting between the Germans and their former allies then spread from Porta San Paolo to other quarters, including Piazza Venezia and Trastevere. The well-armed Germans soon overcame the Italians. An American nun who witnessed the violence recorded this act of charity: an elderly Italian "stooped over a dead body, looked about helplessly, then went across the street and commandeered a fruit seller's handcart, laboriously placed the corpse on it and wheeled it off to the hospital."[10]

Four plaques mounted on the wall to the left of the pyramid honor those who fought to defeat the Germans. The top plaque, dated 1947, praises (in Italian) those who "guided only by faith" showed Italians "the ways of honor and liberty." A second plaque, also in Italian, lauds "the sacrifice of those who died to regain liberty and democracy for Italy, which had been trampled by Nazi-Fascist barbarism." On the right, a third plaque honors Allied troops killed between Anzio and Rome. A fourth plaque, dated 1990 and mounted to the left, commemorates women who fought in the Italian Resistance.

Porta San Paolo is named after Saint Paul, who reportedly walked by this spot on the way to his execution. Parts of the gate date to the third century CE, when a defensive system was built to keep invaders out of Rome. Those fortifications included lofty terracotta brick walls, sections of which still run alongside Via Campo Boario, the street to the left of the pyramid.

Ostiense Train Station

Hours: Best seen in daylight.

Directions/what to see: Across the piazza from Porta San Paolo stands a station built in the 1930s and still used for trains to Ostia and elsewhere. On May 3, 1938, Hitler arrived at this station for a visit with Mussolini and King Vittorio Emmanuele III, who with selected troops welcomed the dictator to Rome. No plaque calls attention to Hitler's visit. However, in memory of Romans deported to concentration camps during the war, five life-size metal figures, chained and handcuffed, line the sidewalk to the station's entrance.

Rome War Cemetery *(Commonwealth)*
Via Zabaglia; http://www.cwgc.org/admin/files/Italy.pdf

Hours: Monday-Friday, 8am–3pm.

Directions: From Porta San Paolo, walk two blocks down Viale del Campo Boario, which runs west from the pyramid. Turn right at Via Zabaglia, a street that goes under a high brick arch. Immediately after the arch, enter the cemetery through a small brick building on the left.

What to see: 429 burials. Within the entrance building, a plaque in English provides a summary of the Italian campaign. The inscription around the building's ceiling honors the long friendship of the British and Italian peoples. The cemetery's grounds are in pristine condition. Most headstones bear a soldier's name, unit, date of death, and age at time of death, with the unit crest carved at the top. Some markers also have a few lines of prose or verse chosen by family or friends. For example, on one is inscribed: "He died that we might live. May we be worthy of his great sacrifice." On another is written: "Our darling Arthur. To live in loving hearts is not to die." Along one wall of the cemetery stands a large stone altar inscribed with these words: "Their names liveth for evermore."

Protestant Cemetery *(Cimitero Acattolico)*
Via Caio Cestio 6; www.protestantcemetery.it

Hours: Monday-Saturday 9am–5pm; Sundays and public holidays 9am–1pm.

Directions/what to see: Exit the War Cemetery and turn left. Take your first right at Via Caio Cestio. Walk several hundred yards to the gated entrance on the right. Although not a World War II site, this historic place (also called the Non-Catholic Cemetery) is worth seeing. The English poets John Keats and Percy Bysshe Shelley are buried here, as well as Antonio Gramsci, a key figure in European Communism.

The Jewish Museum *(Museo Ebraico)* and the Great Synagogue *(Tempio Maggiore)*
Lungotevere Cenci, tel.0668400661; www.jewishitaly.org

Hours: *October–May*, Sunday–Thursday 10am–5pm, Friday 9–2; *June–September*, Sunday–Thursday 10am–7pm, Friday 10am–4pm. Closed Saturdays, Jewish holidays, and January 1.

Admission: €7.5 (includes tour of synagogue); children under 10 free

Directions: Exit the Protestant Cemetery, turn right, and walk the few hundred yards to Via Marmorata. Cross that street and board bus #280 for a ten-minute ride to Piazza Monte Savello, the stop directly in front of the synagogue and very near the Tiber River.

What to see: The Jewish Museum and the synagogue are enclosed by a tall iron gate. Follow signs to the museum information desk, where the schedule of English-language tours is posted. The guide escorts visitors into the synagogue and there summarizes the history of Rome's Jewish community. He/she also describes the construction of this synagogue, which was erected in 1904 and is the largest of Rome's twelve temples. Its splendid interior includes a dome painted in all colors of the rainbow, a symbol of God's covenant with the Jews. Regular services are still held here.

The museum is part of the synagogue. Its six spacious rooms display precious textiles, liturgical vessels, maps, books, and scrolls in large cases. Panels in English, Hebrew, and Italian describe the artifacts, explain the basic tenets of Judaism, and review the history of the Jewish community in Rome.

In the last room of the museum, a film titled *A Star over Rome* describes Jewish history in Rome from 1870 to 1986, with a focus on World War II. Italian and English versions of the film alternate throughout the day. Included in this film is footage that shows the arrest and deportation of Roman Jews to concentration camps in October 1943. This terrible story, also told on panels in the room, can be summarized as follows:

On September 25, 1943, the head of the German SS ordered the Gestapo chief in Rome, Herbert Kappler, to make plans for deporting the Roman Jews to concentration camps. The following day, Kappler summoned two leaders of the Jewish community to his office at Villa Wolkonsky, an estate that is now the residence of the British ambassador. Although Kappler knew that Jews of Rome would be deported regardless of how much gold they collected, he still insisted that the Jewish community hand over fifty kilograms of gold within two days to avoid deportation. The community, working together, collected the demanded amount. The film *A Star over Rome* shows the actual victims making their donations.

The two Jewish leaders brought the gold to Kappler. Nevertheless, the German officer and his subordinates continued making plans to deport the Jews. The Germans' task became easier when they found a card file listing the names and addresses of members in the synagogue office.

On October 6, Fascist police working for Kappler arrested a quarter of Rome's six thousand Carabinieri, the city's elite security force, perhaps in part to keep them from interfering with the deportation of Jews. These fifteen hundred men were sent to forced labor camps in northern Italy or Germany.

On the morning of October 16, German troops began rounding up Jewish men, women, and children. After arresting about one thousand people, the Germans transported them to the barracks of a military school near the Vatican. On October 18, over one thousand Jews were placed in freight cars at the Tiburtina train station. This dreadful event is shown in the film *A Star over Rome*. After six days the train reached a concentration camp in Poland, where most deportees died. Additional deportations of Roman Jews occurred in the following months.

After touring the museum, exit and look at the plaques posted on the exterior walls of the synagogue. One lists the names of Jewish members of the Resistance who died fighting "Nazi-Fascist barbarism." At the bottom of this plaque are engraved (in Italian) these words: "let their sacrifice be a warning to the oppressor and a model for the oppressed." A second plaque honors the six million Jews who died in World War II, a number that includes almost all the 2,019 men, women and children deported from Rome during the occupation. Engraved at the bottom of the plaque is this thought (in Italian): "these are not dry numbers, but a tribute of blood and tears in an injured civilization and an injury to the holy law of God."

Rome *(Part B)*

Travel notes: This chapter's tour takes about a day and a half. It begins with sites that concern the anti-Fascist Resistance and ends at Mussolini's palatial villa. Complete directions for using public transportation are given below. Obtain free street and subway maps from your hotel or a tourist office.

General tourist information in English: http://en.turismoroma.it

Historical summary: A loosely-structured anti-Fascist movement existed in Italy prior to the September 1943 armistice. In the 1930s and early 1940s, Italian anti-Fascists published clandestine newspapers, sheltered political dissidents, and engaged in other activities to undermine Mussolini and his government.

After the Germans occupied Italy in September 1943, the anti-Fascists became more organized. That September, the leaders of six Italian political parties met in Rome to form the CLN, the Committee for National Liberation. This coalition included Socialists, Communists, and several other parties. Regional liberation committees soon formed in other occupied Italian cities, including Milan, Bologna, and Turin. From September 1943 until the end of the war, the CLN served as the umbrella political body for occupied Italy. At the same time, each party retained its own political organization and desire for power in postwar Italy. The Communists were especially aggressive in that regard.

Millions of Italians who opposed the German occupiers participated in the Italian Resistance, which had two major sections. The first consisted of those who used non-violent means to undermine their oppressors. For example, many Italian civilians and clergy sheltered Jews and fugitive Allied POWs. Some acted as spies for the Allies. The second section was called the Armed Resistance and consisted of those who used violent means to attack German and Italian Fascists. Its members commonly were called *partigiani* (partisans). Historians often divide the Armed Resistance into three subgroups: partisan brigades operating under the direction of the CLN, partisan brigades operating without direction from the CLN, and such entities as the FMCR (Clandestine Military Front of the Resistance), which contained many former soldiers.

Partisans captured by the Germans or Italian Fascists often were tortured and sometimes executed. However, on occasion German leaders also punished innocent civilians for attacks carried out by partisans. In parts of occupied Italy in 1944, German soldiers executed anywhere from three to ten Italians for every German killed by a partisan. These massacres were intended to discourage civilians from aiding the partisans and avenge the loss of German lives. One of the deadliest slaughters was carried out in Rome; the details are given below. Large-scale massacres also occurred in rural settlements, such as Sant'Anna (Chapter 8) and Monte Sole (Chapter 11).

SITES
Via Rasella

Hours: Best seen in daylight.

Directions: From centrally-located Piazza Barberini, which has a subway stop, walk one block down Via delle Quattro Fontane and turn right onto Via Rasella, a narrow one-way street.

What to see: On the afternoon of March 23, 1944, an Italian partisan set off a bomb that killed thirty-three men in a group of German and Austrian troops marching up Via Rasella. The surviving soldiers retaliated with gunfire. Damage from that gunfire is still visible on the apartment houses at the intersection of Via Rasella and Via Boccaccio.

What happened here: The planning and execution of the Via Rasella attack involved at least a dozen partisans from an organization called GAP, which stood for Gruppi di Azione Patriottica (Patriotic Action Groups). They chose March 23 for the attack chiefly because that day marked the twenty-fifth anniversary of the Fascist Party's formation.

This assault involved considerable advance work. In a nearby basement, two partisans manufactured the bomb and attached it to a fuse. They then placed the bomb in a trash cart. Another partisan, disguised as a street cleaner, rolled the cart to Via Rasella 155, a handsome Renaissance palace known as Palazzo Tittoni. Ironically, Mussolini had an apartment in this building during the 1920s.

After the bomb was in place, other partisans stationed themselves at various points on the street, ready to give the signal to light the fuse as the troops approached. When they finally appeared and were marching up Via Rasella, a partisan named Rosario Bencivenga lit the fuse and moved quickly away. Less than a minute later, the bomb exploded, killing at least twenty-five people immediately. Partisans stationed nearby then used pistols and hand grenades to kill some of the surviving troops. In all, thirty-three soldiers and several Italian civilians died as a result of this attack.

The remaining troops did not slink away. Guessing that the explosion was caused by bombs thrown from the surrounding buildings, they sprayed those buildings with machine gun fire. Surviving soldiers also dragged residents of Via Rasella from their homes, lined them up, and arrested them. Fortunately, most were freed the next day.

When Hitler heard about this attack on his forces, he became furious and demanded that at least thirty Italians be executed immediately in retaliation for each dead soldier. His subordinates persuaded him that killing ten Italians for each soldier would be sufficient reprisal, and agreed to carry out the executions as quickly as possible.

In Rome, the chief justice of the German military tribunal approved the execution of prisoners already convicted of capital crimes. That group was small. In order to round up at least 330 men by March 24, Herbert Kappler (head of the Gestapo in Rome) added prisoners accused of political crimes and Jews awaiting deportation to his list of "people-to-execute." He also added a man who had been acquitted at trial but not yet released from prison.

Because so many men were to be killed and buried quickly, Kappler decided against using the customary open-air execution site, Fort Bravetta. Instead, he chose a web of caves that could be accessed from Via Ardeatina in the southern part of Rome. With great speed, 335 prisoners were transported to the caves and executed in groups of five by German soldiers. To bury the bodies, German engineers then mined and blew up the entrances to the tunnels, creating a huge mass grave.

On March 25, 1944, newspapers in Rome carried a brief announcement that 335 Italians had been executed in reprisal for the Via Rasella attack, but did not indicate who had been killed or where the bodies were. The final sentence of the announcement simply noted that the executions had been carried out.

The next two sections describe a former prison (now a museum) whose inmates were executed in this massacre, and the massacre site itself. In memory of the 335 men killed there, the caves have been renamed the Ardeatine Graves.

History Museum of the Liberation
(Museo Storico della Liberazione)
Via Tasso 145, tel. 067003866; www.viatasso.eu

Hours: Tuesday, Thursday, and Friday, 9:30am–12:30pm and 3:30pm–7:30pm; Wednesday and weekends, morning hours only.

Directions: From Via Rasella (described above), return to Via Quattro Fontane and turn left. Walk back to Piazza Barberini and take the subway (*metro*) to Viale Manzoni. Walk over one block on Via Labicana and turn left on Via Tasso. A sign marks the entrance to the museum.

If you prefer to walk from Via Rasella, return to Via Quattro Fontane and turn right. That street soon becomes Via De Pretis. Continue straight on Via De Pretis for four blocks to Piazza Esquilino, which is dominated by the Basilica of Santa Maria Maggiore. Walk to the front of that basilica and take Via Merulana for six blocks to Via Alfieri. There turn left and walk over two blocks to Via Tasso.

What to see: This museum occupies several floors of a building used by the Germans as a prison during the occupation. The men imprisoned here in late March 1944 were executed at the Ardeatine Caves.

First floor: These rooms were offices for the Germans during the occupation. Now they serve as a library, archive, and auditorium. On the auditorium walls hang maps that illustrate the expansion of a Resistance group (the Clandestine Military Front) in Italy between 1943 and 1944. Next to the maps hang photographs of Italian intellectuals and officers who fought against Fascism. Another wall exhibits a priest's account of a Roman anti-Fascist group.

Second floor: Five rooms formerly used as prison cells. **Cell 1** has photos with biographies (in Italian) of men killed at the Ardeatine Caves. **Cell 2** is the size of a large closet; it was used for solitary confinement and remains as it was during the occupation. Messages scratched by prisoners are still visible on the plaster walls. Examples are: "La morte è brutta per chi la teme" (Death is an evil for the person who fears it); "Medita o uomo sulla tua nullità di fronte alla grandezza dell'universo" (Man, meditate on your nothingness in comparison with the grandeur of the universe). **Cell 3** displays the music and lyrics of a lullaby written by an imprisoned priest for an inmate whose wife was pregnant. Also displayed are prison records and photographs of Fort Bravetta, a military installation on the western outskirts of Rome that the Germans used for executions. In addition, **Cell 3** exhibits a page from the diary of Mario De Martis, a 23-year-old prisoner whom the Germans executed at Fort Bravetta. In that page, translated below, De Martis described his life at Via Tasso:

> *10 April 1944*
> *After fourteen days I begin this diary of mine, hoping in my heart to end it soon by regaining my liberty. I could say many things about the fourteen days that I've lived here, but would rather omit those and consider only what will happen from now on. I'll start by talking about my cell. It's on the second floor and marked with the number 5. It has a radiator that's always off, a light that's always on, a door and window firmly shut—with the window bricked-up, of course. Two wooden benches serve as beds for two of the lodgers selected for the longest stay in this inaccessible place, which is as easy to enter as it is hard to leave. Here it's necessary to spend the interminable hours of the day and night, to count the minutes of these hours and the seconds of these minutes, one by one. So life passes monotonously and uniformly: night follows day, day follows night. With the first rays of dawn and the first sun we open our eyes, and with our eyes we open our hearts to hope. Today is the fourteenth [day of] useless hope.*

The second floor has two additional cells. **Cell 4** exhibits photographs of La Storta, a suburb to the north of Rome. Here fleeing German soldiers executed fourteen prisoners taken from Via Tasso on the day that the Allies marched into Rome. The Germans then continued their retreat north. **Cell 5** was for solitary confinement. Colonel Giuseppe Montezemolo was imprisoned in this room for months prior to his execution at the Ardeatine Caves on March 24, 1944. Montezemolo had served in the Italian Army until the 1943 armistice, when he became head of the Clandestine Military Front of the Resistance. In that role he provided information to Allied commanders and acted as a liaison between the royalist underground and other clandestine groups in Rome. The Germans captured Montezemolo in January 1944. Although tortured, he never revealed the names of his associates or any other secrets. A letter posted in the room thanks Montezemolo's widow for his assistance to the Allies.

   Third floor: Rooms formerly used as cells. Prisoners' sketches and writings are still visible on the narrow cell used for solitary confinement. On one wall, a prisoner scratched a British flag with the phrase "England Forever" on the flag's base. The remaining third-floor rooms display wartime posters with messages directed at Rome's citizens. For example, a poster dated September 14, 1943, warns Romans to hand in their weapons and not help the partisans. Exhibited also are samples of the underground newspapers produced by the Italian Resistance.

The third floor also hosts the Shoah Memorial Room, which displays documents about the persecution and deportation of Roman Jews. This room was created in cooperation with the Survivors of the Shoah Visual History Foundation.

Ardeatine Graves *(Fosse Ardeatine)*
Via Ardeatina 174, tel. 065136742. The history of this site is discussed above in the section on Via Rasella.

Hours: Daily 8:30am–3:30pm.

Directions: From the Via Tasso museum, walk two blocks to the large piazza in front of the Basilica of St. John Lateran (San Giovanni in Laterano). There board bus #218, the only public transportation to the Ardeatine Graves, which lie several miles south of the basilica. Bus #218 takes about twenty minutes to reach its stop in a parking area on the right side of Via Ardeatina. Walk one block down that street to the site's entrance.

The ancient catacombs of San Callisto are near the same bus stop and also are open to the public.

What to see: Just past the entrance gate stands the supervisor's office, where brochures in English and other languages are provided. Opposite the office, a massive sculpture portrays prisoners as they died here, handcuffed and bound. This monument stands in a circular courtyard that acts as an anteroom to the caves, which are high-ceilinged, well-lit, and easy to traverse.

Within the caves, a path leads visitors to a site map and small chapel. The executions occurred further down the path, in an area now shielded by gates. A large plaque posted on the cave wall notes (in Italian): "Here were slain victims of a horrible sacrifice. May from our sacrifice rise a better nation and lasting peace among peoples." A plaque also marks where German engineers detonated explosives to block access to the caves.

Additional signs point the way outdoors to the mausoleum. This massive stone structure shelters 335 tombs, each engraved with the name, age, and occupation of the person executed. Most also have a photo of the victim. The tombs are arranged in sixteen rows, with walkways every second row. Outside the mausoleum, a stone staircase leads to a small museum that displays photographs of Rome during the occupation and newspaper accounts of this massacre. Behind the museum are well-kept gardens.

Basilica of St. John Lateran
(Basilica di San Giovanni in Laterano)
Piazza San Giovanni

Hours: Daily 7am–7pm.

Directions/what to see: From the Ardeatine Graves, take bus #218 back to the basilica, which is the center of a large Roman Catholic complex. During the early months of the occupation, the adjoining seminary provided shelter for Jews and anti-Fascist dissidents. Thousands more fugitives found refuge in other churches, convents, monasteries, and church offices, including those across from the nearby Basilica of Santa Maria Maggiore. Italian civilians also provided sanctuary in their homes.

Huge statues of saints adorn the top of San Giovanni's façade. During the occupation, an inebriated German soldier mistook those figures for Allied soldiers and shot at them.

San Giovanni has a magnificent interior and is well worth a visit. Attached to it are a cloister and papal museum, which have small admission fees and more limited hours.

Memorials in the Via Veneto Neighborhood

Hours: Best seen in daylight.

Directions/what to see: If you are coming from the Basilica of San Giovanni, take the subway to the Barberini stop and walk north through Piazza Barberini to Via Veneto.

Many visitors to Rome stay near Via Veneto, a wide boulevard lined with five-star hotels and upscale shops. This famous street also had many luxury hotels before World War II. During the occupation, the Germans requisitioned these hotels for lodgings and took over nearby buildings as offices. Plaques and a statue near Via Veneto mark a Nazi tribunal and a prison run by Italian Fascists.

To reach the former Nazi war tribunal, walk to the intersection of Via Veneto and Via Boncompagni, site of the American Embassy. Go two blocks east on Via Boncompagni and turn right at Via Lucullo, where a bronze statue and plaque flank the entrance of building #7. The Italian inscription on the plaque means: "During the ill-starred occupation, the Nazi war tribunal in this building tried in vain to suffocate in blood the Roman people's craving for freedom." To the left of the doors, a life-size statue, cast in 1986, portrays a man who has been tied up and beaten to death. The Italian inscription next to the statue begins: "Here the lives of men were squandered by the ferocity of Nazism."

To reach the memorial marking a former Fascist prison, return to Via Boncompagni and turn right. Walk three blocks to Via Romagna and turn left. A plaque at #38 Via Romagna notes (in Italian) that Fascist officers, led by the sadistic Pietro Koch, tortured their captives in the building that used to stand at this site. Contemporary accounts support that claim. An American nun living in Rome noted in her diary that the prison on Via Romagna was "fitted up with the same hideous instruments as the one in Via Tasso: pincers for pulling out teeth and fingernails, whips, rods, and means of heating knives red-hot. Some of our friends who live near there and hear the screams and groans, particularly at night, say it is diabolical."[11]

Villa Torlonia *(Mussolini's Home)*

Via Nomentana 70, tel. 0682059127; http://en.museivillatorlonia.it/

Hours: Open daily except Monday at 9am, with these closing times: *April–September* 7pm; *March and October* 5:30pm; *November–February* 4:30pm; closed January 1, May 1, and December 25.

Admission: Free to the grounds; Casino Nobile €4.5; Casina delle Civette €3

Directions: From the memorial on Via Romagna (described above), walk four blocks south to Via XX Settembre. Cross that busy street and take any eastbound bus (#36, 60, 62, 84, or 90) for about ten blocks to the intersection of Via Nomentana and Via Torlonia, where gates mark the entrance to the villa. An information booth within the entrance sells tickets to selected buildings and offers brochures in English.

What to see: From 1925 until July 1943, this estate was the home of Mussolini and his family, who leased it for a trivial sum from a noble Roman family. The villa's lovely grounds are open at no charge to the public. Magnolias, palms, cedars, and chestnut trees enliven the landscape and provide shelter on hot days. Restful spots include a casual restaurant with indoor/outdoor seating and a children's playground.

The city of Rome acquired Villa Torlonia in 1978 and has recently restored the mansion, called Casino Nobile. Its three floors are open to visitors. Frescoes, paintings, and statues adorn the first floor's elaborate rooms. Panels in English and Italian explain these works of art. Some of the statues date back to the Roman Empire and were found on the estate during the current restoration. Additional panels summarize the history of the Torlonia family, whose ancestors built this complex in the nineteenth century.

A first-floor room displays photos of Mussolini and his family using the villa's pool and tennis court. Another snapshot shows the dictator riding a horse, his regular morning exercise. Displayed also are photographs of the lavish wedding reception given at the mansion for Mussolini's daughter.

Mussolini hosted many famous individuals at Villa Torlonia, such as the emperor of Ethiopia, Haile Selassie, and even Hitler himself. In 1931 Mahatma Gandhi was a guest for a few days and startled his hosts by bringing a goat.[12]

Some of the dozen or so other buildings within the estate are in the process of being restored and so may be viewed only from the outside. However, visitors may enter the Casina delle Civette (Cottage of Owls). This building has a whimsical exterior. Its interior gleams with early twentieth-century stained glass designed by Cesare Picchiarini, a master of that art.

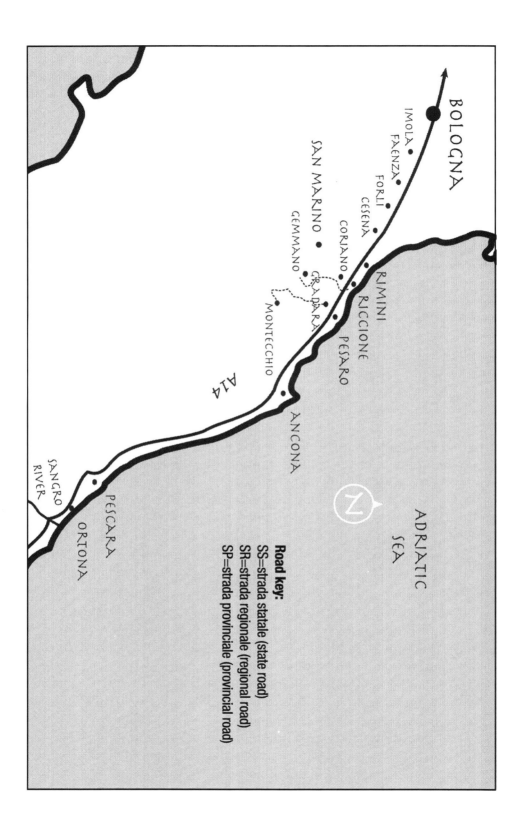

BOLOGNA

IMOLA
FAENZA
FORLI
CESENA
SAN MARINO
CORIANO
GEMMANO
GRADARA
MONTECCHIO
RIMINI
RICCIONE
PESARO
A14
ANCONA
SANGRO RIVER
PESCARA
ORTONA

ADRIATIC SEA

N

Road Key:
SS=strada statale (state road)
SR=strada regionale (regional road)
SP=strada provinciale (provincial road)

From Ortona to Rimini, and on toward Bologna

Travel notes: This chapter concentrates on the advance of the Eighth Army along the Adriatic Coast and across a section of the Po Valley. The complete tour takes several days and crosses three regions of Italy: Abruzzi, Marche, and Emilia-Romagna. A car is necessary to reach most sites.

The Eighth Army was commanded by British generals and drew most of its units from nations of the British Commonwealth, including (in the Italian campaign) the United Kingdom, Canada, New Zealand, India, South Africa, and Rhodesia. It also contained units from Poland, Nepal, Greece, and elsewhere. The precise makeup of this army varied over the course of the campaign, as did that of the Fifth Army.

General tourist information in English:
Marche: www.le-marche.com
Emilia-Romagna: www.emiliaromagnaturismo.it/english/
Rimini: www.riminiturismo.it/rimini/guida/eng/monumenti.htm
Forlì and Cesena: www.turismo.fc.it
Imola: http://en.comune.imola.bo.it

Historical summary: After the conquest of Sicily in the summer of 1943, the Eighth Army crossed over to the Italian mainland in early September. It then advanced north along Italy's Adriatic coast, seizing the air base at Foggia and the city of Bari. By the middle of December 1943, Canadian troops at the front of the Eighth Army had reached Ortona, a coastal city occupied by German troops. The enemies clashed for nine days outside that city, with many casualties on both sides. Canadian troops finally won that terrain, but the Germans still held the city. Canadian and German soldiers then battled within Ortona in fierce door-to-door battles. After a week, the Germans retreated. These battles damaged or destroyed most of Ortona's buildings and ravaged the surrounding countryside.

At the end of December, General Bernard L. Montgomery halted the Eighth Army in order to conserve resources for the spring campaign. Montgomery then handed over command of that army to General Oliver Leese and flew to England to prepare for the invasion of France, scheduled for mid-1944.

In the spring of 1944, most of the Eighth Army moved to the area around the city of Cassino, where the Fifth Army was trying to overcome German forces (see Chapter 2). At the end of May, those two armies finally broke through German defenses at Cassino; in June and July, they advanced north through Lazio and into Tuscany. At the same time, the Germans were making a measured retreat to their best-fortified positions in northern Italy, which were called the Gothic Line. This "line" was a series of bunkers, trenches, gun turrets, land mines, and other defenses installed across the Apennine Mountains, from La

Canadian soldiers prepare grave crosses near Baranello, Italy, October 1943.
Library and Archives Canada

Spezia on the Ligurian coast to near Pesaro on the Adriatic. Its purpose was to prevent or at least slow the advance of Allied forces.

The rugged terrain north of Florence contributed to a change in Allied strategy. The commanders knew that the Eighth Army had few mountain troops but was well supplied with tanks and artillery. They thus decided that most of the Eighth Army should move back to the Adriatic coast (where the hills are lower), break through the Gothic Line south of Rimini, and then advance across the flatlands from Rimini to Bologna. This move eastward involved tens of thousands of men and vehicles traveling over damaged mountain roads.

Once in position, the Eighth Army began its offensive on the night of August 25 (1944) near the Metauro River, which flows into the Adriatic near the city of Pesaro. By dawn, all divisions had crossed the river and were advancing up the coast. The strength and speed of their attack surprised the Germans, who soon shifted troops from the center of Italy to meet this assault.

Over the next few days, Eighth Army forces pushed north and west, penetrating as much as twenty miles inland from the coast. During this time, thousands of soldiers died and many villages were destroyed. The historian Douglas Orgill noted that in some villages, the only men left after the battles were those "who would never leave. They sat, wedged side by side, in the ruined cellars of the old stone houses; sprawled in piles in the doorways of barns; lay in untidy heaps in the little peasants' houses where they had crawled to die."[13]

Eighth Army troops took the city of Pesaro on September 2, 1944, thus breaking through the Gothic Line at its easternmost point. They then continued their advance, taking one ridge after another. By September 19, troops were battling on the outskirts of Rimini, a city already devastated by Allied bombardments. This seaside haven suffered more damage when the Germans attacked its port facilities.

Rimini fell to the Eighth Army on September 21. Some troops then advanced north toward Ravenna, which was taken by Canadian forces in December. Other Eighth Army divisions were transferred to France. The remaining forces advanced west along SS9 (also known as Via Emilia) toward Bologna. This road traverses the Romagna plain, an area crossed by a dozen or so rivers flowing from the mountains to the sea. Heavy autumn rains had swollen these streams and turned earth to mud, making it difficult for tanks and trucks to advance.

For three months, Eighth Army troops fought their way across rivers and soggy fields, liberating Cesena, Forlì, Faenza, and other towns as they advanced. Land mines planted around rivers by the Germans made those crossings more perilous than expected. In the end, shortages of supplies, stiff enemy resistance, and severe weather prevented Eighth Army soldiers from reaching Bologna before winter. They thus halted and entered winter quarters near the city of Faenza at the end of December 1944.

FROM ORTONA TO RIMINI
Museum of the Battle of Ortona
(Museo della Battaglia dell'Ortona)
Corso Garibaldi, Ortona, tel. 0859068207; http://muvi.org/muba

Hours: Monday–Friday 9am–1pm; also 3pm–6pm Tuesday and Thursday.

Directions: By car from Rome, take expressways A24 and A25 across Italy. Near Pescara (on the Adriatic Coast), exit on to expressway A14 southbound and get off at Ortona. The road winds through an industrial zone for several miles before reaching the city's busy center. Follow signs to Corso Garibaldi, the street that runs along the harbor. The museum overlooks the water and is part of a cultural complex that includes a theater and public library. On-street parking is free in spaces marked with white lines.

What to see: This museum displays photographs taken shortly after the battle for Ortona. These show various scenes, such as citizens standing in the rubble of their homes and Canadian soldiers aiding civilians. Captions are in English and Italian. Also exhibited are weapons, uniforms, and other military equipment. A small shop sells postcards and books about the battle. Free tours are offered in English, Italian, and German. The museum website provides a virtual tour.

Memorials in Piazza Plebiscito

Hours: Best seen in daylight.

Directions/what to see: After exiting the Ortona museum, turn right and continue along Corso Garibaldi for six blocks to Via Guicciardini. There turn left and walk the four blocks to Piazza Plebiscito. In the middle of that piazza stands a statue group that depicts a soldier caring for a wounded comrade; its title is *The Price of Peace*. Nearby, a large plaque honors the Canadian troops that fought at Ortona.

Commonwealth War Cemeteries

www.cwgc.org./admin/files/Italy.pdf

Hours: Open daily during daylight

Directions: Individual directions are given below. Italian road signs and maps often identify a Commonwealth cemetery as *cimitero inglese.*

What to see: These cemeteries honor the Eighth Army troops that fought and died near the following locations in 1944. Most headstones bear a soldier's name, unit, date of death, and age at time of death; the unit crest is carved at the top.

- **Sangro River:** 2,617 burials; a cremation memorial honors an additional five hundred Indian Army soldiers. This cemetery is about fifteen miles south of Ortona. Exit expressway A14 at Val di Sangro. After 1.5 miles, turn right onto SS16. Drive another mile and turn right, following signs to the cemetery.

- **Moro River:** 1,615 burials, the majority Canadian soldiers. Exit expressway A14 at Ortona and take SS16 south, following signs for San Donato. The approach road to the cemetery passes through an archway connected to the church of San Donato.

- **Ancona:** 1,029 burials. Exit expressway A14 at Ancona Sud (South). Take SS16 toward Ancona for two miles and turn right. Pass under a railway line and turn left at the next junction. Follow that road for a few miles to the cemetery, which is on the left, just past a gas station.

- **Gradara:** 1,192 burials. Exit expressway A14 at the sign for Cattolica (between Pesaro and Riccione) and follow signs for the village of Gradara. The cemetery lies on a terraced hillside a few miles outside Gradara, which contains a renovated castle open to the public.

- **Montecchio:** 582 burials. From Gradara (or from Pesaro), follow signs for the town of Montecchio. The cemetery lies across from a roundabout on the town's main street.

Gothic Line Museum *(Museo della Linea dei Goti)* at Montegridolfo

Via Roma 2, tel. 0541855320; www.montegridolfo.eu (click on "Guida alla visita" for an English version)

Hours: *May–October 15,* Sundays 4pm–7pm. *October 16–April,* Sundays 3pm–6pm. By appointment Monday–Saturday.

Directions/what to see: From Montecchio (or from Pesaro), follow signs to the pretty village of Montegridolfo, where the war museum borders a luxury hotel/restaurant complex. Displayed are weapons, gas masks, cigarette cases, and other items left by soldiers in the area, as well as contemporary photographs and newspapers.

War Memorials in Gemmano

Hours: The photographs may be seen weekday mornings.

Directions: Exit expressway A14 at Riccione and follow signs west to Coriano (described below). From Coriano, drive about eight miles south to Gemmano. Both towns were devastated during the war and have been rebuilt.

What to see: Gemmano's town hall (*municipio*) dominates its hilltop piazza. Opposite town hall, several open-air memorials commemorate area battles. An eloquent poem about war (in English, Italian, and German) is inscribed on the base of a fifteen-foot statue of a soldier. Next to the statue, a large mosaic indicates where local battles were fought.

Within town hall (open weekday mornings), forty or so large framed photographs depict Gemmano before, during, and after the war, thereby documenting the intensity of area combat. In September 1944, the Germans initially held the heights along the Gemmano Ridge, and did not yield without a struggle. According to historian Douglas Orgill, "all around the bullet-chipped cross on Point 449, the dead, khaki and field-grey, lay heaped, unburied, in score upon score; at their centre a soldier of the Lincolns whose hands were still frozen in death around the cross itself."[14]

Eighth Army forces ultimately did gain control of this area, but at great cost to both sides. James Speer, a British captain, visited Gemmano after the battle and reported that one large house was "packed with corpses. The wind on the top of the ridge was blowing straight through the house from front to back, and all the broken shutters were banging, but there was no other sound. . . . When the wind dropped, it was absolutely quiet. That's what I remember most, the quiet and the smell."[15]

Coriano War Cemetery *(Commonwealth)*

www.cwgc.org./admin/files/Italy.pdf

Hours: Open daily during daylight.

Directions: From Gemmano, follow signs north for eight miles to Coriano. The cemetery stands a mile outside town on a secondary road to Rimini and is surrounded by cultivated fields.

What to see: 1,939 burials. Magnolia trees line the cemetery's perimeter and shade some graves. Most headstones bear a soldier's name, unit, date of death, and age at time of death; the unit crest is carved at the top. As in other Commonwealth cemeteries, a plaque provides details in English about local battles. This rural area, now so peaceful, was filled with the smoke and roar of combat in September 1944. Many men died in the battle to take the Coriano Ridge, the last major hill group before Rimini.

FROM RIMINI TOWARD BOLOGNA

Rimini is a vibrant city filled with art treasures. In summer, tourists jam its beaches, clubs, and restaurants. Like many coastal cities, Rimini experienced tremendous growth in the postwar years. As you tour this prosperous place, it may be hard to imagine that Rimini was severely damaged during the war. At that time, many civilians took refuge in the nearby city-state of San Marino, which today offers various tourist attractions.

Piazza Tre Martiri *(Three Martyrs)*

Hours: Best seen in daylight.

Directions/what to see: Rimini's central square is named after three Italian men whom the Germans accused of sabotage and executed in August 1944. The plaque on the piazza's tall clock tower honors additional local partisans. A few blocks from this piazza stands the historic Malatesta Temple, a Renaissance church damaged by bombs during the war and repaired years ago.

Rimini Gurkha War Cemetery *(Commonwealth)*

www.cwgc.org./admin/files/Italy.pdf

Hours: Open daily during daylight.

Directions/what to see: 618 burials and a memorial to the 170 men whose remains were cremated. From the center of Rimini, drive several miles on SS72 toward San Marino. Turn right at the small sign to the *cimitero* (cemetery) and follow the signs. Pass through a rectangular brick building into the well-maintained grounds, where most headstones are inscribed with a man's name, unit, date of death, and age at time of death; the unit crest is carved at the top. Gurkha soldiers, natives of Nepal, were known for their courage and tenacity in battle.

Aviation Museum *(Museo dell' Aviazione)*

Via S. Aquilina 58, Rimini, tel. 0541756696; www.museoaviazione.com

Hours: Open daily at 9am with these closing times: *July–August* 7pm; *March–June and September–October* 6pm. *Winter* by appointment.

Admission: €10 July and August; €8 the rest of the year

Directions/what to see: From the Rimini Gurkha cemetery, continue for a few miles on SS72 toward San Marino. Turn right at the sign for the museum, which sits on a hillside and provides ample parking. The museum consists of two parts, an outdoor and indoor exhibit. Displayed outside are military aircraft and aviation artifacts from World War II and later periods. American, Soviet, and Italian manufacturers are represented. Panels next to each item provide historical information in English and Italian. The indoor museum, set in a metal farm-style building near the entrance, displays photographs, small pieces of equipment, flight logs, letters, documents, and uniforms.

Commonwealth War Cemeteries
www.cwgc.org./admin/files/Italy.pdf

Hours: Open daily during daylight.

Directions: Individual directions are given below. Italian road signs and maps often identify a Commonwealth cemetery as *cimitero inglese.*

What to see: These cemeteries honor the Eighth Army troops that fought and died near the following towns in the fall of 1944. As elsewhere, most of the headstones are inscribed with a man's name, unit, date of death, and age at time of death. The unit's crest is carved at the top.

- **Cesena:** 775 burials. Exit expressway A14 at Cesena. Follow Via Cervese several miles to a roundabout and turn left onto Via Spinelli. Take the next left at the "Hera" recycling center, which borders the road leading to the cemetery. *If you have come to Cesena by train*, this site is an easy walk from Cesena's station. Turn left as you exit the station and walk to the end of the block. Following the signs, go through the underground passageway to the other side of the tracks. Continue straight on Via Cervese for four blocks. At the first traffic circle, turn right on Via Spinelli. Take the first left after the "Hera" recycling center to reach the cemetery.

- **Forlì (Indian):** 496 burials and a memorial to the 768 soldiers whose remains were cremated. Exit expressway A14 at Forlì and follow SR67 (also known as Via Ravegnana) south toward the city center. This site is on the left, opposite the municipal cemetery.

- **Forlì:** 738 burials. From the city center, drive south on SS67 to a sign for the village of Vecchiazzano, where the cemetery lies on Via delle Forze Alleate (Allied Forces Street).

- **Faenza:** 1,152 burials. Exit A14 at Faenza and follows signs to SS9 (also known as Via Emilia). Drive east for a short distance on SS9 and turn at the sign to the cemetery, which lies about a mile southeast of the city.

In addition these war cemeteries, the towns between Rimini and Bologna have interesting sites unrelated to the war. At Cesena stands the splendid fifteenth-century Malatesta Library. Forlì has a picturesque fortress and several historic churches. Faenza welcomes visitors to the International Museum of Ceramics, whose collections include ceramics created by Matisse, Chagall, and Picasso.

A Walk through Imola
The city of Imola is thirty minutes from Faenza by train or car. Its World War II sites relate to the German occupation, which lasted from September 1943 until April 1945. For a tour of those sites, please see the last section of Chapter 7.

Sites between Florence and Imola

Travel notes: This chapter provides three related itineraries. The first describes locations in or near Florence that can be seen in a day by using public transportation.

The second tour, which requires a car and takes about two days, follows the route of the Fifth Army from Florence north toward Imola and Bologna. The Fifth Army consisted chiefly of American forces, but also contained British units and French colonial troops.

This chapter closes with a half-day walking tour of historic sites in Imola.

If you have time to make a side trip from Florence to western Tuscany, two of that area's major war sites are described in Chapter 8.

General tourist information in English:

Florence: http://firenzeturismo.it/en.html
Tuscany: www.tuscany.org; www.mugellotoscana.it
Emilia-Romagna: www.emiliaromagnaturismo.it/english/
Imola: http://en.comune.imola.bo.it

Historical summary: In late May 1944, Allied victories south of Rome compelled German troops to withdraw from Rome and other cities in central Italy. Over the summer, German forces tried to block or at least slow the advance of the Allies, but by August 1944 Allied soldiers were approaching Florence. German troops blew up most of the city's historic bridges just before the Allies arrived.

When the Germans abandoned Florence in August 1944, they also withdrew from other locations in Tuscany and Umbria for a measured retreat to their best-fortified positions in northern Italy, known collectively as the Gothic Line. This "line" was not a wall, but rather a series of bunkers, anti-tank trenches, gun turrets, land mines, and other fortifications installed across the Apennine Mountains, from La Spezia on the west coast to near Pesaro on the Adriatic. These defensive structures, built by forced labor, were meant to block or at least slow the advance of Allied troops.

The mountainous terrain north of Florence contributed to a change in Allied strategy. The Eighth Army had few mountain troops but was well supplied with tanks and artillery. Allied commanders thus decided that most of the Eighth Army should move to the Adriatic Coast, where the hills are lower, and break through the Gothic Line just south of Rimini. To the Fifth Army was given the task of breaking through the Gothic Line in the central and western Apennines.

In September 1944, while the Eighth Army was battling along the Adriatic, the Fifth Army began its assault on the center of the Gothic Line. Key points were two mountain passes through which roads ran from Florence to Bologna: the Futa Pass (near the village of Traversa) and the Giogo Pass. General Mark Clark, the Fifth Army's commander, learned that the Futa Pass was better fortified and so directed his troops' chief effort toward the Giogo Pass.

The approach to the Giogo consisted of a winding narrow road flanked by mountains, from which German gunners could observe the Allied advance. German planners had tried to make these mountains impassable by constructing "pillboxes and dug-outs, some of them blasted from the solid rock," which were positioned to "support each other up the side of the mountains. The standard type held about six men and was constructed of concrete, with a roof covered with three feet of logs and soil, and a firing slit six inches high and three feet long."[16]

For eight days in the middle of September, Allied and Axis troops clashed on Mount Altuzzo and other peaks near the Giogo Pass. Although the Allied forces numbered over 262,000 men, historian Ernest F. Fisher noted that this rugged terrain did not allow for grand attacks by "coordinated formations." As a result, the men who would bear the "brunt of the fighting at critical points sometimes constituted a platoon or less, seldom more than a company or two. Little clusters of men struggled doggedly up rocky ravines and draws separated by narrow fingers of forested ridges, isolated, climbing laboriously squad by squad, fighting their way forward yard by yard, often not even knowing the location of the nearest friendly unit."[17]

Chronicles of the battle for the Giogo Pass cite many instances of heroism, such as the actions of an American soldier, Private Oscar G. Johnson. The only unwounded man in his squad, he crawled around the battleground to gather ammunition and for hours kept firing on the enemy, thus almost single-handedly protecting the left flank of his company's position. For the full story, see the Congressional Medal of Honor Society website.

By September 18, Allied troops overcome German forces and held an area seven miles wide on either side of the Giogo Pass. The Germans were retreating north toward the town of Firenzuola and did little to block the Fifth Army's advance. By September 22, other Fifth Army divisions broke through the Gothic Line at the Futa Pass, where they had encountered relatively little opposition. Thus at the end of September, these divisions were in position to advance north through still more mountains.

When Fifth Army troops reached the town of Firenzuola, General Clark ordered three divisions to continue on to Bologna. However, he sent the U.S. 88th Infantry Division toward Imola, a city about thirty miles east of Bologna. The plan was to trap German troops between wings of the Fifth and Eighth Armies.

On September 21, U.S. 88th Division troops began their advance, meeting little enemy resistance as they took one mountain peak after another. They shelled the village of Castel del Rio as they approached, which caused the Austrian soldiers holding it to withdraw, but also damaged the village's buildings.

On September 27, Italian partisans guided some American soldiers to their next objective, Monte Battaglia (Battle Mountain). To their surprise, the Germans seemed to have abandoned this strategically important peak. However, the peace was short-lived. American troops had scarcely settled on Monte Battaglia when the Germans began an all-out attempt to retake its heights.

The fighting went on for a week. With the help of additional British and American units, the U.S. 88th Division prevented the Germans from recapturing this peak. This victory was costly. Over two thousand men of that division were killed or wounded between September 21 and October 3. Afterward, the U.S. 88th Division did not continue on to Imola, but rather moved west to join other Fifth Army divisions advancing toward Bologna. The Allies had hoped to capture that city before winter. However, shortages of men and supplies as well as fierce German resistance delayed their advance. Allied troops thus entered winter quarters a short distance from Bologna in December 1944.

The conquest of the Gothic Line was an important milestone in the Italian campaign, and its cost was great. Allied casualties in September and October 1944 were higher than at any other time during the entire Italian campaign.[18]

FLORENCE

German troops occupied Florence in September 1943. During the occupation, this city experienced less physical damage than others. Its preservation in part was due to the efforts of the German consul, as the author David Tutaev describes in *The Consul of Florence*. However, in Florence as elsewhere, there was great human suffering. German troops rounded up and deported Jewish citizens. They also imprisoned, tortured, and sometimes executed local partisans.

Museum of Jewish Art and History *(Museo dell' Arte e Storia Ebraica)* and the New Synagogue *(Nuovo Tempio)*
Via Farini 4 & 6, tel. 055245252; www.jewishitaly.org

Hours: Fridays 10am–2pm. Sunday–Thursday, open at 10am with the following closing times: *April–May and September–October*, 5pm; *June–August*, 6pm; *November–March*, 3pm. Closed January 1 and all Jewish holidays.
Admission: €5 adults; €3 students (includes guided tour of the synagogue)

Directions: From the main train station, walk three blocks on Via Nazionale to Via Guelfa. Turn right and walk nine blocks to Via Farini; turn left. The museum and synagogue stand behind gates in the middle of the block.

What to see: This magnificent synagogue, the fifth largest in the world, was built in the late nineteenth century. The Germans used it as a warehouse and stables during the occupation. After the war, the building was restored to its former glory. A massive stone block in its front garden bears the names of 248 Jews deported from Florence to concentration camps. The actual number of deportees is said to be greater. Names are added as they are discovered.

The museum contains objects and documents that illustrate the history of Florence's Jewish community from its beginnings in 1437 to modern times, including many photographs.

Bridges over the Arno River
Hours: Best seen in daylight.

Directions/what to see: From the central train station, walk through Piazza Santa Maria Novella to Via dei Fossi. Continue down that street for two blocks to the reconstructed Ponte Santa Trinità, one of the bridges destroyed by German troops before they abandoned Florence (only Ponte Vecchio was spared). Cross Ponte Santa Trinità. On the left, a plaque notes that the bridge was built in 1569, destroyed by German mines on August 4, 1944, and rebuilt between 1955 and 1957.

Florence War Cemetery *(Commonwealth)*
On State Road (SS) 67; www.cwgc.org./admin/files/Italy.pdf

Hours: Daily 8am–4:30pm.

Directions: Board city bus #14 on Via della Scala, a street that runs along one side of Florence's central train station. Via della Scala eventually runs into SS67. Get off at the last stop, Il Girone, where there is a bus shelter. Walk one block more down SS67 to the cemetery, which has a parking area in front. The whole trip takes about twenty minutes.

What to see: 1,632 burials. Rows of headstones and cypress trees lead to a marble memorial overlooking the Arno River and forested hills. Most of the headstones are inscribed with an individual's name, unit, date of death, and age at time of death. The inscriptions reflect the diversity of the Commonwealth, with soldiers from Britain, Canada, India, Nepal, and elsewhere. The names of the Indian Army and Gurkha troops are written both in English and the script of their native language.

Florence American Cemetery
Via Cassia; www.abmc.gov/cemeteries/cemeteries/fl_base.pdf

Hours: Daily 9am–5pm; closed January 1 and December 25.

Directions: The cemetery lies about eight miles south of Florence on Via Cassia, the road to Siena, and can be reached by public bus. Check its schedule at the SITA bus station on Via Santa Caterina di Siena, half a block from Florence's central train station. If you prefer to drive, take Via Cassia to the cemetery, which provides ample parking.

What to see: 4,402 burials. This beautifully-maintained cemetery covers seventy acres and occupies a peaceful location overlooking forested hills. Near the entrance, a reception center provides free brochures in English. To see a particular grave, ask the superintendent about the books and online sources that show where each person is buried. Most headstones bear an individual's name, rank, native state, and date of death. For those whose bodies could not be identified, the marker notes: "Here rests in honored glory a comrade in arms known but to God." Paths lead up through the rows of graves to monumental open buildings whose walls display maps of the Italian campaign and the names of soldiers missing in action. Veterans, civilians, and soldiers gather here to pay tribute with speeches and hymns on the United States' Memorial Day, the final Monday in May.

FROM FLORENCE TO IMOLA

This itinerary follows the advance of the Fifth Army from Florence north through the Giogo Pass. Well-known battlegrounds include Monte Altuzzo and Monte Battaglia.

War Museum at Scarperia

www.goticatoscana.it

Directions/what to see: From Florence, drive north on SR65. Go through the town of San Piero a Sieve and continue north on SP503 to the town of Scarperia, where a war museum is scheduled to open in 2010. For news in English about the museum and related military re-enactment activities, visit the above website.

Monuments near the Giogo Pass *(part of the Gothic Line)*

Hours: Best seen in daylight.

Directions/what to see: About halfway between Scarperia and the Giogo Pass, a large monument to the 363rd Regiment of the U.S. 91st Division stands just off SP503. Signs point the way to this memorial, which is set on a small hill. Visible from this site are the mountains that blazed with the roar and smoke of war when the Fifth Army broke through German lines at the Giogo Pass in September 1944.

Continue driving on SP503 to reach the Giogo Pass and Mount Altuzzo, in whose shadow stands a monument dedicated to the 338th Regiment of the U.S. 85th Division, also part of the Fifth Army.

Visit **www.progettolineagotica.eu** for information in English on efforts to preserve the Gothic Line fortifications.

German Military Cemetery *(Deutscher Soldatenfriedhof/ Cimitero Militare Germanico)* at Traversa

Hours: Daily, *December–February*, 9am–4pm; *March and October*, 8am–5pm; *April– September*, 8am–7pm.

Directions: From the Giogo Pass, drive north on SP503. Near the town of Firenzuola, continue west on SP503, following signs for SR65 *southbound* toward the Futa Pass. Stay on SR65 to the cemetery, which lies a mile south of the village of Traversa. Signs in German and Italian indicate the parking area.

What to see: 30,173 burials. In the entrance building, free brochures provide information in English, German, and Italian about this vast graveyard, which was built in the 1960s. Many of the men buried here were killed defending the Gothic Line. In contrast to Allied cemeteries, each headstone lies flat on the ground and bears the names of two or more individuals. The ten thousand or so granite markers are arranged in spirals on mountainside terraces. At the top of the mountain stands a fortress-like building that contains memorials to various German units. The views of the surrounding peaks are spectacular.

Santerno War Cemetery *(Commonwealth)* at Coniale

www.cwgc.org./admin/files/Italy.pdf

Hours: Open daily during daylight.

Directions: From the German cemetery, return on SR65 and SP503 to Firenzuola. There follow signs for SP610 and drive seven miles north toward the village of Coniale. The cemetery lies on the right, about a mile past the village. Its parking area is rough but adequate.

What to see: 287 burials. As in other Commonwealth cemeteries, most headstones are inscribed with a soldier's name, unit, date of death, and age at time of death. The grave markers of French-Canadian soldiers bear dedications in French.

War Museum *(Museo della Guerra)* in Castel del Rio

Piazza della Repubblica; www.museodellaguerradicasteldelrio.it

Hours: Sundays 2pm–6pm.

Admission: € 2.5; children under 10 free

Directions/what to see: From Coniale, continue north on SP610 for seven miles to the village of Castel del Rio. The museum is in Palazzo Alidosi, a centrally-located Renaissance palace that formerly belonged to the Alidosi family. It displays weapons, uniforms, medals, military radios, and other items found on nearby battlefields. Near the ticket desk hang photographs of a battlefield monument that honors an American officer, Lieutenant Colonel Charles Furr, and the soldiers of the 351st Regiment, U.S. 88th Division. Furr was killed while leading an advance patrol near Castel del Rio. The mountain pass where he died is called Il Passo del Colonnello (Colonel's Pass). Furr's family dedicated this memorial on September 24, 2000.

Castel del Rio was devastated by wartime shelling. In late 1944 a British civil governor was appointed to supervise the rebuilding of the area; his headquarters were in Palazzo Alidosi. Today the village contains many picturesque stone buildings, some of them fairly new.

Across from the museum entrance, a paved road runs down to a park and a bridge (*ponte*) that spans the Santerno River. Ponte Alidosi was built in 1499, named a national monument in 1897, used by troops during the war, and is still in use today. Its appearance is striking: a single arch high above the river, with a span that seems to float in space. Rooms within the bridge are open to the public on Sunday afternoons.

Monuments on Battle Mountain *(Monte Battaglia)*

Hours: These sites must be visited in daylight.

Directions/what to see: Drive five miles northeast from Castel del Rio on SP610 to the village of Fontanelice. Following signs for Monte Battaglia and La Rocca (the fortress), turn at Via Dante Alighieri and drive uphill on a paved road for six miles to a gravel path near the peak. Park and walk the short distance to a brick terrace, near which lie massive statues of two Old Testament figures: David resting on his shield after killing Goliath, and the broken fragments of Goliath's head. These statues symbolize the struggle between Italian partisans (David) and German soldiers (Goliath). Other memorials include a plaque posted on the remains of a medieval fortress. The plaque's inscription, written in German, English, and Italian, honors all who died here. Another plaque offers this prayer in Latin: "Once enemies, now friends, let us pray for peace in the world." The views from the peak are spectacular.

Vestiges of War in Tossignano

Hours: These sites must be visited in daylight.

Directions/what to see: From Fontanelice, drive northeast on SP610 to the town of Borgo Tossignano. In the town center, turn right on Via XX Settembre and continue uphill on the paved road for three miles to the village of Tossignano. Just before the village is a small park with a large bronze statue of a soldier. This World War I memorial, erected in 1928, also has a plaque honoring soldiers and civilians killed in World War II.

Like many other Italian villages, Tossignano was severely damaged during the war. Some of the rebuilding in its central piazza is recent. For example, a plaque on a stately new palazzo notes that the building formerly on this site was destroyed during the war and finally replaced in 2000. To the left of that palazzo stands a handsome church. To the left of the church is a new information center called I Gessi e Il Fiume (Chalk Hills and the River) after the area's natural attractions. This center is open on Sundays.

During the war, German troops dug tunnels and stored weapons beneath the remains of a nearby medieval castle. To reach this site, walk from Tossignano's central piazza up a one-lane flagstone street called Via San Michele. Pass by several houses to reach a modern church named Santa Maria Assunta. Next to the church is a convent, Villa Immacolata. Walk past the convent and continue uphill for several hundred yards to the remains of the castle. A huge metal cross towers over the ruins, beneath which German soldiers dug tunnels. These heights offer fine views of the countryside.

A WALK THROUGH IMOLA

Imola is about twelve miles by car from Tossignano and about thirty minutes by train from Bologna. Its chief World War II sites relate to the occupation, which ended when Eighth Army troops liberated Imola in April 1945. Most of these sites can be seen at any time. However, the fortress and Resistance Center are **not** open daily.

From Piazza Matteotti to Chiesa del Carmine

Directions/what to see: Begin this mile-long tour in **Piazza Matteotti**, the city's central square, where both German and Italian Fascists maintained headquarters during the occupation. In this piazza on April 29, 1944, a rally to protest food shortages ended in bloodshed when Fascist soldiers opened fire on the crowd, killing two women, Livia Venturini and Rosa Zanotti. A plaque on the façade of Palazzo Comunale commemorates their deaths.

To the left of that memorial hang two larger plaques. One carries the presidential decree that gave *Medaglia d'Oro* (Gold Medal) status to the citizens of Imola for their resistance to the German occupation. A second plaque praises the local partisan group, the 36th Garibaldi Bianconcini Brigade, for constituting "a continuous threat to the back of the enemy and an aid to the Allies in the area of the Gothic Line" while "bombardments, oppressions, deportations, and massacres" rained down on Imola. The Garibaldi brigade consisted of one thousand armed partisans who clashed with the Germans and aided the Allies in and around this city.

Branching off from Piazza Matteotti is the **Street of the Jews (Via dei Giudei)**, a narrow lane that displays a plaque placed by the city of Imola and the Jewish community of Bologna. This plaque notes (in Italian) that Jews settled here during the fourteenth century and had a synagogue nearby until 1567, but were expelled from Imola at the end of the sixteenth century. It also says that despite the anti-Semitic racial laws passed by the Italian government in 1938, Imola's citizens tried to protect local Jews, especially during the occupation.

From Piazza Matteotti, walk east under a large brick arch and continue a block down Via Emilia to the corner of Via XX Settembre. At that corner stands a four-story building built during the early 1930s. Known then as **Palazzo del Fascio,** it is now called Centro Cittadino (Civic Center). Its façade still displays inscribed sentences from a speech given by Mussolini in 1936. In the (Italian) inscription, the dictator harps on a favorite theme, the rebirth of the Roman Empire:

> *Italians have created the Empire with their blood. They will make it resound with their toil and defend it with their weapons against everyone. Legionnaires, in this absolute certainty lift high your banners, swords, and hearts to salute the reappearance of the Empire on the fateful hills of Rome after fifteen centuries. Will you be worthy of it? This cry is like a sacred oath that binds you before God and men through life and through death.*

Beneath the inscription, images of workers in Fascist Italy, such as soldiers and blacksmiths, decorate the stone columns. The dates on this building follow the Fascist method of counting from 1922, the year Mussolini began his rule. Thus the year of construction, 1933, is written as XI, and Mussolini's speech is dated "9 maggio 1936 XIV dell'era fascista" (May 9, 1936, the fourteenth year of the Fascist era).

From the Palazzo del Fascio, continue east on Via Emilia. The fifteenth-century palace marked 132–140 is **Palazzo Volpe**, which served as barracks for troops from Mussolini's new army. At Via Emilia 80 stands **Palazzo dei Musei**, home to some of Imola's fine art museums and its public library. A block farther down Via Emilia, at the corner of Via Fratelli Cairoli, is **Chiesa del Carmine**. This church and convent complex served as a refuge for Jews, partisans, and former Allied POWs during the occupation. Fugitives hid in the complex's basements, bell tower, and spaces accessible through trap doors.

The Fortress *(La Rocca)*

Hours: Saturday 3pm–7pm; Sunday 10am–1pm and 3pm–7pm. See the Imola website for special openings: http://en.comune.imola.bo.it.

Admission: €3

Directions/what to see: From Chiesa del Carmine, cross Via Emilia and walk over two blocks on Via Fratelli Bandiera to this imposing fortress, where anti-Fascists were imprisoned during the war. Brochures available at the entrance describe the history of the fortress, parts of which date to the thirteenth century. This structure was enlarged by fifteenth-century rulers and restored in the late twentieth century. It now displays collections of Renaissance weapons, cannons, and armor.

Documentation Center for the Antifascist Resistance *(CIDRA)*
Via dei Mille 26, just off Piazza Mirri

Hours: Tuesday, Thursday, and Saturday 9:30am–noon and 3pm–5:30pm; closed in August.

Directions/what to see: From the fortress, walk back through Piazza Matteotti to reach this center. Its seven rooms display wartime maps, posters, and photographs, including snapshots of city buildings devastated by bombs. The center also serves as a research library and gathering place for veterans.

American pilot signals to his ground crew before taking off from his base in Italy, September 1944.
U.S. National Archives

American soldiers pass ammunition as they battle near Lucca, November 1944.
U.S. National Archives

Lucca and Western Tuscany

Travel notes: The two sites described in this chapter are in rural settings about eighty miles northwest of Florence and less than thirty miles from the city of Lucca. A good way to reach these sites is to take the train from Florence to Lucca, and there rent a car.

Lucca is famous for its architecture, music festivals, and cuisine.

General tourist information in English: www.luccaturismo.it

SITES

Gothic Line fortifications at Borgo a Mozzano

www.luccaturismo.it (enter the phrase "Borgo a Mozzano" in the search field). The best-preserved remains of the Gothic Line cluster around that town.

Hours: A few of the fortifications, such as an anti-tank wall, are easy to find and may be seen at any time. However, to visit the interiors of bunkers and other remains of the Gothic Line, you must book a guided tour at **proloco@borgoamozzano.org**. Local volunteers give tours in Italian on the second and fourth Saturday of most months, usually in the mornings. It may be possible to arrange a tour in English.

Historical summary: Laborers began installing defensive structures at the coastal towns west of Lucca in the late 1930s, the time when Italian officials began preparing for war. Plans also were made to construct a series of fortifications across Italy, from La Spezia on the west coast to the town of Fano on the Adriatic. These fortifications, eventually named the Gothic Line, consisted of bunkers, trenches, gun turrets, land mines, anti-tank walls, and other structures placed at vulnerable points across the Apennines. Their purpose was to help stop or slow the advance of enemy troops.

In October 1943, the Todt Organization assumed supervision of the Gothic Line. This organization was named after Fritz Todt (1891–1942), who supervised the building of the German highway system and other infrastructure projects in the 1930s.

From November 1943 until August 1944, local workmen and laborers from elsewhere "volunteered" to work on the fortifications near Borgo a Mozzano, often as a means of avoiding prison or deportation to Germany. These men built dozens of tunnels, bunkers, and trenches between Borgo a Mozzano and a village to its south, Piaggione. They also planted land mines, installed barbed wire, and constructed a huge anti-tank wall.

These workmen were divided into groups of one hundred and supervised by armed guards. Some laborers slept in barracks near Borgo a Mozzano. The guards and Todt officials requisitioned private houses in that town for their living quarters, and used Palazzo Giorgi on Via Regina Margherita and Palazzo Santini in Piazza San Rocco for their offices. Both buildings were equipped with bomb shelters.

The Allies learned about these fortifications from a young Italian surveyor named Silvano Minucci, who infiltrated the Todt Organization and copied selected maps. Minucci recruited a young Italian woman to carry these maps to Fifth Army leaders.

Directions/what to see: From Lucca, take highway 12 north to the exit for Borgo a Mozzano and follow signs toward the town center. On the right, about a mile before the center of town, the massive concrete anti-tank wall looms over an empty field. A few hundred yards closer to town, several large information panels stand on the left side of the road. These panels display photographs, maps, and notes in English about the history of the Gothic Line. They also flank the entrance to one of several wartime bunkers, which are kept locked to prevent damage and inappropriate use. The bunkers are well-lit and display military items found in the area.

Sant'Anna di Stazzema National Park of Peace
(Parco Nazionale della Pace)
www.santannadistazzema.org (click on British flag for English version)

Hours: This national park and its monuments commemorate civilians executed by German soldiers. The park is open daily. Its museum has limited hours: *June 1 to September 30*, Thursday–Saturday and Tuesday, 9am–7pm; Wednesday and Sunday 2:30pm–7pm; closed Mondays. *Other months*, check the website.

Historical summary: During the summer of 1944, German troops were battling the Allies and also trying to round up Italian recruits to serve in labor camps or Mussolini's new army. At the same time, Italian partisans were working to undermine the Germans and aid the Allies. As the partisans increased their attacks, German commanders adopted extreme measures in hope of crushing this resistance. Part of their strategy included executing civilians in reprisal for assaults carried out by partisans. It is estimated that the Germans killed several thousand women, children, and elderly people in Tuscany alone during 1944.

In the Lucca area during 1944, partisan brigades were cutting telephone lines, attacking German supply vehicles, and killing soldiers. German troops attempted to arrest these men, but most escaped capture. German commanders then decided to carry out reprisals against the area villagers, some of whom were thought to be aiding the partisans. One of the villages chosen as a massacre site was Sant'Anna di Stazzema.

On August 12, 1944, two hundred German troops gathered the residents of the hamlets around Sant'Anna and brought them into the village. They then massacred over five hundred people, including infants, children, women, and the elderly. Some were herded into the cottages and killed with hand grenades. Other victims were shot in front of the village church. In the weeks before and after this event, the Germans killed smaller number of civilians in other nearby villages.

Years after the war, monuments were erected at Sant'Anna and elsewhere to keep the memory of these massacres alive. In 2004, ten former German soldiers were accused of participating in the killings at Sant'Anna and put on trial *in absentia* at La Spezia, a city near Lucca. On June 22, 2005, Italian judges convicted and sentenced these men to life in prison. At this time the men remain in Germany, which does not extradite its citizens.

Directions: Sant'Anna is thirty miles northwest of Lucca. From there, take expressway A11 west toward Viareggio. Exit onto expressway A12 north toward Genoa. Exit A12 at the sign for Camaiore and follow signs to that town. Once you are within Camaiore's narrow streets, follow signs to the slender road that runs uphill through the villages of La Culla and Santa Lucia. Two and a half miles before Sant'Anna, a scenic overlook provides a place to stop and read English-language information panels. The entrance to the park is well-marked.

What to see: Sant'Anna has only a few residents at this time. Begin your visit in the church, which displays photographs of the children killed in the August 1944 massacre. Listed also are the names of local priests murdered by the Germans during the summer of 1944.

A stone monument on the lawn in front of the church notes (in Italian) that "hundreds of men, women, and children" were killed here "for no other reason than that they had sought refuge in the mountains." This monument also names three other sites where many civilians were massacred during the war: Lidice, Oradeur, and Marzabotto. The memorials at Marzabotto are described in Chapter 11 of this guide.

A small museum is set in the former village school next to the churchyard. It displays large photographs of individuals who survived the massacre and their accounts (in Italian) of that horrific experience. Translations of these stories are being prepared. The museum also exhibits wartime photographs of local partisans and Allied soldiers.

Near the museum, a trail called "Via Crucis" (Way of the Cross) runs uphill to a lofty stone tower. Along the trail stand sculpted panels that show Christ on his path to crucifixion. These panels are paired with images of the massacre at Sant'Anna.

At the top of the mountain, the eighty-foot memorial tower shelters statues of a murdered woman and infant. The tower's base contains the remains of victims slaughtered on August 12, 1944. A plaque lists the names of those who could be identified.

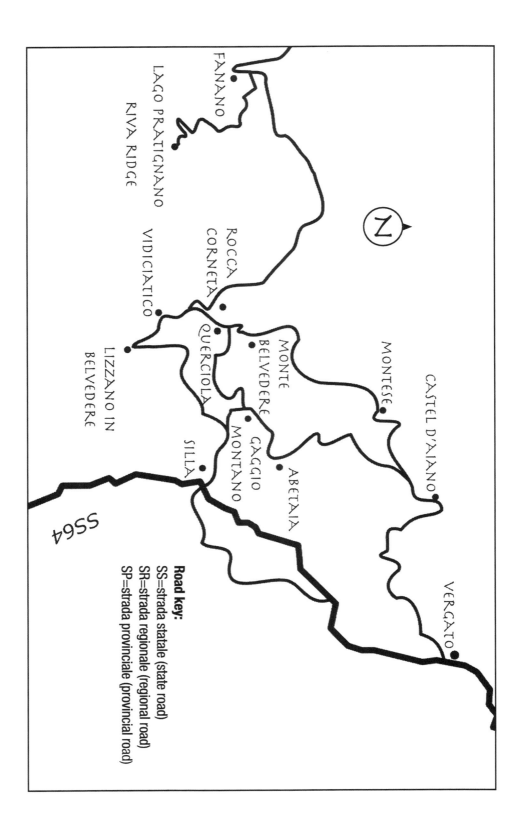

Road Key:
SS=strada statale (state road)
SR=strada regionale (regional road)
SP=strada provinciale (provincial road)

N

SS64

FANANO

LAGO PRATIGNANO

RIVA RIDGE

VIDICIATICO

ROCCA
CORNETA

QUERCIOLA

MONTE
BELVEDERE

LIZZANO IN
BELVEDERE

SILLA

GAGGIO
MONTANO

ABETAIA

MONTESE

CASTEL D'AIANO

VERGATO

Sites between Lucca and Bologna

Travel notes: To reach all sites described below, you will need a car and two or three days; twisting roads in this mountainous area make the driving slow. Several hikes to wartime sites are outlined below. Those who want to do more hiking can buy trail maps in local book stores or on-line. The maps published by Edizioni Multigraphic (titled *Sentieri C.A.I. e Percorsi Trekking*) are widely sold in Italy.

General tourist information in English:
www.emiliaromagnaturismo.it/english/

Historical summary: The summer of 1944 was a time of change for the Fifth Army. In August 1944 it lost seven divisions and other units to a long-planned assault on southern France. Assigned to fill their places were the U.S. 92nd Infantry Division and the Brazilian Expeditionary Force, which had 25,000 men. In early September, the U.S. 92nd Division contributed to the liberation of Lucca. Its 370th Regiment then set up an outlook post in the cathedral's bell tower, while other troops established a perimeter defense around the city. Engineers worked to restore Lucca's water supply, which had been sabotaged by the Germans.

The U.S. 92nd Division next advanced toward SS64, the main route from Pistoia (a city just west of Florence) to Bologna. In the fall of 1944, German forces held the peaks that overlook SS64 and thus could control this important supply/communication route and its feeder roads. That fall, Fifth Army forces tried to drive German troops from these mountains, but did not succeed in doing so.

In January 1945, the arrival of the U.S. 10th Mountain Division created a second chance to seize these strategically important peaks. This well-equipped division had trained for mountain warfare in the Rockies before coming to Italy. Once they arrived in the Apennines, one of their first goals was to drive the Germans off Riva Ridge, a series of peaks halfway between Lucca and Bologna.

On the night of February 18, after days of on-site preparation, five U.S 10th Mountain Division assault parties began the climb up the southeastern side of Riva Ridge. Its sheer slopes were considered impregnable by the German troops encamped on its heights. However, the 10th Mountain Division soldiers successfully made this very difficult ascent and, after reaching the top at dawn, took some Germans prisoner. German troops soon counterattacked, and fierce fighting ensued. Two days later, 10th Mountain Division engineers finished building a tramway that was used to transport supplies and wounded men between the top and base of the mountain. By February 25, Allied troops had driven the last German soldiers from Riva Ridge.

When the attack on Riva Ridge was underway, additional 10th Mountain Division troops fought to seize Mount Belvedere and other mountains from German forces. These attacks sometimes required soldiers to climb through open terrain, making them easy targets for enemy gunfire. In his first-hand account, 10th Mountain Division veteran Robert Ellis noted that he and his comrades could not "predict when or where the unseen enemy artillery would drop the next shell," making it impossible to time moving "across the killing ground to try and escape death."[19] Despite these difficulties, 10th Mountain Division soldiers took Mount Belvedere and other crucial peaks by the beginning of March. About the same time, the Brazilian Expeditionary Force captured Mount Castello. Thus, by March 5, Allied forces held a six-mile front from the village of Castel d'Aiano to SS64, the road to Bologna.

SITES
Riva Ridge Battlegrounds

Hours: This climb must be done in daylight.

Directions: U.S. 10th Mountain Division soldiers captured Riva Ridge from the Germans in February 1945. The hike to the top of one of its peaks, Mount Serrasiccia, can be done in a day. The mountaintop has panoramic views and several war memorials.

To reach Riva Ridge from Lucca, drive east to the city of Pistoia and take SS64 northbound (if driving to Riva Ridge from Bologna, take SS64 southbound). Exit SS64 at the sign for Silla. Drive through the towns of Silla, Gaggio Montano, and Rocca Corneta, where signs for the town of Fanano begin to appear.

About two miles before Fanano, look on the left for a sign to the information center called Due Ponti (Two Bridges). Turn left at the paved road that runs to the center, which is open on weekends. Drive past the center and cross a small bridge, following signs for Lago (Lake) Pratignano, which is at the top of Mount Serrasiccia. Hairpin turns make the drive uphill very slow.

Keep driving until the paved road turns to gravel. Although it is possible to continue by car, it's more interesting to park and hike the rest of the way. Two scenic routes are available: the gravel road and CAI (Club Alpino Italiano) trail #405. Trail #405 runs behind the stone house that overlooks the point where the paved road becomes gravel. Both the road and trail run uphill past groves of trees and ancient stone cottages with collapsing roofs. The hike is between two and three miles.

What to see: At the top of Mount Serrasiccia is a cleared area of several acres. In the clearing stand two memorials: a bronze plaque dedicated to all who fought in these mountains in 1944 and 1945, and a panel with photographs of Allied soldiers resting in this very spot. Nearby are a picnic area and a large bog-like lake, Lago Pratignano. CAI trail #401 continues past the lake and goes along the ridge to other mountains in the chain. There are splendid views from those peaks.

Memorials in Querciola

Hours: Best seen in daylight.

Directions/what to see: From Riva Ridge, drive back through Rocca Corneta and follow signs to the village of Querciola. In its center, opposite the church, a monument topped by a cross pays tribute to all victims of war. Next to this monument, Italian-language posters describe the battles at Riva Ridge and Mount Belvedere. About a block from the church, a piazza named after the U.S. 10th Mountain Division has two life-size statues that represent an American and an Italian mountain soldier. In 1988, a group of local *Alpini* (Italian mountain soldiers) dedicated this work, sculpted by Andrea Pizzuti, to the 10th Mountain Division.

German Fortifications on Mount *(Monte)* Belvedere

Hours: This climb must be done in daylight.

Directions/what to see: From Querciola, follow signs north toward the village of Montese. About a mile from Querciola, small wood and metal signs on the right mark the entrance to a single-lane paved road. Turn right, drive uphill for a short distance, and turn left into a small gravel parking lot when the road forks. Park and walk around the gate to an unpaved road that leads uphill for about half a mile. When that road forks, turn left and continue walking for about fifteen minutes to the top of the mountain, where the extensive remains of a German camp lie next to the ruins of a castle. A posted diagram sketches the settlement and identifies various structures, such as shelters, trenches, rifle emplacements, storage areas, and living quarters. It is easy to see from this elevation why having the higher position is an advantage in battle.

Brazilian War Monument near Gaggio Montano

Hours: Best seen in daylight.

Directions/what to see: From Querciola, drive through Gaggio Montano toward the village of Abetaia. About half a mile before that village, signs on the left mark the single-lane paved road to the monument. Drive up this road a few hundred yards to the thirty-foot abstract sculpture, which stands in the middle of fields and was created by the artist Mary Vieira to honor Brazilian forces. Its title is *Liberation: A Single Volume in Free Rhythm*. In the distance looms Mount Castello, which Brazilian troops captured from the Germans in 1945.

History Museum of Montese *(Museo Storico di Montese)*
Via della Rocca, tel. 059971127; www.museo.comune.montese.mo.it

Hours: *July and August,* Monday–Saturday 4pm–6pm; Sunday 11am–1pm and 4pm–7pm. *April–June and September*, same hours, Saturday and Sunday only. *October–March*, Sunday 11am–1pm and 3pm–5pm.

Admission: €2

Directions: From Gaggio Montano, follow road signs to the village of Montese. Park in Montese's central piazza and there look for posted signs to Museo Storico, which is set in the ruins of a medieval fortress (La Rocca) about half a mile from the piazza. Follow those signs up several narrow streets and past the village church, San Lorenzo. From there, continue uphill to the museum.

What to see: The first two rooms of this museum concern local history and culture. In Room I, maps show the locations of nearby historic churches and castles. Room II displays equipment used to make local products, such as cheese and wine casks. Other rooms exhibit weapons, uniforms, skis, and ice picks used by the U.S. 10th Mountain Division. Also displayed are life-size model battleground scenes, such as a replica of the tramway used to transport supplies and wounded soldiers at Riva Ridge. In addition, several rooms honor the achievements of the Brazilian Expeditionary Force, which was based in Montese.

Return to Montese's central piazza. From there, walk one block down Via Panoramica to a large stone sculpture that depicts wartime scenes. Representatives of the Brazilian Expeditionary Force donated this monument in 2005.

Memorials and Models at Castel d'Aiano

Hours: The memorials may be seen any day; the Gothic Line model is displayed on Saturdays at 5pm.

Directions/what to see: From Montese, drive northeast for four miles, following the signs for the village of Castel d'Aiano. In its central piazza, across from town hall, a huge plaque lists the names of local citizens killed by the Germans. Behind town hall stands a monument dedicated to all civilians and soldiers who "fought, suffered and died in order to free this land from the tyranny of dictatorial oppression." Among the American soldiers wounded near Castel d'Aiano was Robert J. Dole, who went on to become a U.S. senator and the Republican nominee for President in 1996. Senator Dole now is active in the program that brings veterans to the World War II memorial in Washington DC.

In Castel d'Aiano's Civic Center (Sala Civica), a multimedia model of the Gothic Line is presented on Saturdays at 5pm. To see it, drive from the central piazza down Via Bologna for half a mile. Turn right at Via Val d'Anera, where there is a gas station, and pass a playground. Take the next right into a parking lot and enter the Civic Center, a modern one-story building on Via Val d'Anera. The room-size model illuminates the Gothic Line battles in sequence, along with video clips, sound effects, and a narrative in Italian; an English version is being prepared. The presentation takes forty-five minutes. For more information in English on the Gothic Line, visit **www.progettolineagotica.eu.**

Bologna

Travel notes: Bologna has one of Europe's oldest universities and is a vibrant city with a rich cultural life. Its World War II memorials and museums are easy to reach on foot or by public bus. These sites are grouped into two half-day tours.

General tourist information in English: http://iat.comune.bologna.it

Historical summary: Bologna was (and is) a major transportation hub and industrial center for Italy. The Allies repeatedly bombed this city between July 1943 and the end of the war in order to disrupt the Germans' use of Bologna's rail system and factories. Tragically, these bombings also killed 2,481 civilians.

Due to its political and geographic prominence, Bologna served as a center for the Resistance during the war. On several occasions partisans fought with German soldiers in the city center, perhaps most famously at a city gate called Porta Lame, only blocks from the train station. Today two statues of partisans have been placed at Porta Lame to commemorate that battle.

During the fall of 1944, the Fifth Army and the Eighth Army advanced toward Bologna from points east, south, and southwest of the city, battling German troops much of the way. In late 1944, both sides settled into winter quarters less than fifty miles from Bologna. By that time it was clear the Allies were going to win the war. Under discussion was when and how the Germans would surrender.

In February 1945, the commander of the German SS forces in Italy contacted the chief of American intelligence, Allen Dulles, to begin secret negotiations for the surrender of German forces in Italy. At the same time, both sides continued preparing for the spring offensive. The Germans set up several defensive lines around Bologna. The Allies brought in supplies of ammunition and also weapons not previously used in the Italian campaign.

In early April 1945, the Allied offensive began. Allied pilots dropped thousands of bombs on German positions near Bologna. At the same time, Eighth Army troops launched an assault from the area east of the city. Several days later, Fifth Army forces began their advance from points south and southwest of Bologna. Although some German troops fought back, many abandoned the struggle and surrendered or fled.

On April 21, partisan brigades and Eighth Army troops marched together down Bologna's streets to its central square, Piazza Maggiore. Contemporary photographs show huge crowds of citizens welcoming them along the way and in the piazza. Elsewhere in northern Italy, Resistance leaders proclaimed April 25 a day of general insurrection. In some towns and cities, partisans took control of governing before Allied troops arrived.

A small group of partisans dealt quickly with Mussolini, whom they arrested with his mistress on April 27. The next day they executed the pair and hung their bodies, along with those of other senior Fascist leaders, in Piazzale Loreto, a square near Milan's central train station. During the first week of May, Allied commanders met with their German counterparts to accept the surrender of German forces in Italy.

IN THE CENTER OF BOLOGNA
Memorials in Piazza Nettuno

Hours: Best seen in daylight.

Directions: This busy square adjoins Piazza Maggiore and is named for the huge statue of Neptune in its center. Piazza Nettuno and Piazza Maggiore are in the heart of Bologna and ten blocks from the main train station.

What to see: During the occupation, the Germans displayed the bodies of executed prisoners along the façade of Palazzo Comunale, the municipal building that borders one side of Piazza Nettuno. Many of those executed were accused of participating in the Resistance. After the war, relatives paid tribute to their dead by leaving flowers and photos here. Later, formal memorial plaques were placed on the façade of Palazzo Comunale. These begin on the far left, where a stone plaque is dedicated (in Italian) to the "children, women and men of every race that Nazi ferocity savagely killed in the concentration camps." To the right of this plaque are individual photographs of 2,052 local citizens who died fighting the Germans. Another plaque states that 14,425 members of the Armed Resistance, organized in sixteen brigades, were operating in the Bologna area between 1943 and 1945. Of these, the plaque notes that 2,059 died in combat, 2,350 were executed in reprisal killings, and 829 died in Nazi prisons.

To the right of the palace's central doors, a third plaque honors the thousands of Italian soldiers and officers killed in Cefalonia and Corfu shortly after the September 1943 armistice between Italy and the Allies. These men, after refusing to surrender to the Germans, were killed in battle or executed by firing squads. A fourth plaque awards *Medaglia d'Oro* (Gold Medal) status to the citizens of Bologna for their wartime valor.

Across from Palazzo Comunale stands Palazzo Re Enzo, whose façade has three plaques related to World War II. From left to right, the first celebrates the Italian troops that fought under Allied command and reached Bologna in April 1945. The second plaque honors the six hundred thousand Italian soldiers imprisoned by the Germans after the armistice, here called "martyrs" of the Nazi camps. The third plaque is dedicated to the Italian divisions stationed in Montenegro at the time of the armistice. These forces joined Tito's Yugoslav partisans.

Palazzo dell' Archiginnasio
Piazza Galvani 1 (just off Piazza Maggiore); http://iat.comune.bologna.it (click on "English" and then "museums")

Hours: Monday–Friday 9am–6:45pm; Saturday 9am–1:45pm.

What to see: This building, one of the top tourist sites in Bologna, hosted the University of Bologna from the mid-sixteenth century until 1803. In 1838 it became a library, a role it still plays. Beautiful frescoes adorn the palace's spacious interior halls and conference rooms.

On the second floor, visit the historic Anatomical Theater, where students once sat in carved wooden stalls to watch dissections on a marble operating table. On January 29, 1944, Allied bombs devastated the palace, its Anatomical Theater, and nearby churches, including San Petronio and San Giovanni in Monte. These buildings were repaired after the war, but photos on the theater door show the effects of the bombings.

Air Raid Signs

Hours: Best seen in daylight.

Directions/what to see: On a few buildings in central Bologna, wartime advisory signs are preserved. From Archiginnasio (or Piazza Maggiore), walk through Piazza Galvani to Via Farini. Turn right to see these words painted on the façade of Via Farini 6: "RICHIESTA DI SOCCORSO DURANTE LE INCURSIONI AEREE." This message, which tells where to seek help during air raids, remains also on buildings at Via Santo Stefano 45 and Via San Vitale 23.

Jewish Museum *(Museo Ebraico)*

Via Valdonica 1/5, tel. 0512911280; www.museoebraicobo.it (click on "English")

Hours: Sunday–Thursday 10am–6pm, Friday 10am–4pm.

Admission: €3

Directions: From Piazza Maggiore, walk the long block down Via Rizzoli to the landmark Two Towers (Due Torri). From there, walk two blocks north on Via Zamboni to Via Carro. Turn left on Via Carro and make an immediate right onto Via Valdonica. The entrance is well-marked; press the buzzer to open the gate.

What to see: The museum provides English and Italian audio guides that take visitors through its six rooms. The exhibits concentrate on the history of Jewish culture in Emilia-Romagna. Panels and touch screens provide information in English and Italian. Of particular interest is a map that shows where synagogues still exist in Emilia-Romagna, and where they have been closed. The museum store stocks numerous English-language books.

Museum of the Resistance
(Museo della Resistenza di Bologna)

Via Sant'Isaia 20, tel. 0513397250

www.museodellaresistenzadibologna.it (click on the British flag for the English version)

Hours: *September–June,* Monday–Friday 4pm–7pm and Saturday 10am–1pm. *July and August*, Monday, Tuesday, and Thursday 4pm–7pm and Wednesday/Friday 10am–1pm.

Directions: From Piazza Maggiore, walk five blocks west on Via Ugo Bassi and turn left at Piazza Malpighi. Continue south through the piazza and turn right onto Via Sant'Isaia. Walk two blocks to the museum, which will be on your left.

What to see: This museum is in a renovated former convent that also houses Bologna's History Institute (Istituto Storico). Those two organizations work together to collect, preserve, and exhibit materials concerning Fascism and the Resistance. Four rooms of the museum display photographs of partisans with explanatory texts in Italian. In the fifth room, an Italian-language film depicts Resistance activities in Bologna. For example, the film shows how partisans hid in the city's underground passageways to escape capture.

Italian partisans stand with an Allied medic, 1945.
Frank J. Davis Collection, Southern Methodist University

ON BOLOGNA'S OUTSKIRTS
Memorial Museum of Liberty *(Museo Memoriale della Libertà)*
Via G. Dozza 24, San Lazzaro (a suburb of Bologna), tel. 051461100.
www.museomemoriale.com

Hours: Open by appointment; write to **info@museomemoriale.com** or call the museum office, whose hours are weekdays 10:30am–1pm and 3pm–6:30pm.

Admission: €5

Directions: This museum adjoins two war cemeteries and is easy to reach from the center of Bologna by public bus. The trip takes about fifteen minutes. Take bus #19 *eastbound* from its stop on Via Rizzoli, halfway between Piazza Maggiore and the two landmark medieval towers. Ask the driver to let you off at the stop near the Polish War Cemetery, which borders the museum. Cross Via Dozza and walk left for several hundred yards to a cluster of palm trees flanked by huge vases. Those trees mark the entrance road for the museum, whose buildings occupy several acres. The total distance from the bus stop to the museum's parking lot is about a third of a mile.

What to see: This museum has a variety of exhibits in large warehouse-style buildings. Perhaps most striking are the five life-size scenes that recreate wartime events with special effects and contemporary artifacts. In the first scene, German officials force Italian civilians to work for the Todt Organization, which supervised the construction of the Gothic Line defenses across northern Italy (see also Chapter 8). In the second scene, an Italian family huddles in a shelter while bombs whistle overhead. The third scene depicts that family's house destroyed by bombs. In the fourth, German and Italian Fascists search for partisans in Bologna. The fifth scene portrays U.S. 10th Mountain Division soldiers seizing a German observation post on Riva Ridge, a group of mountains southwest of Bologna (see Chapter 9).

Other buildings exhibit vintage American, British, German, and Italian vehicles, including tanks, trucks, and jeeps. The museum also hosts shows for vehicle collectors. Check the website for the dates of those meetings.

Near one hall sits a boxcar used to transport Jews to concentration camps. Posters hung inside the boxcar depict the horrors of those camps.

Bologna War Cemetery *(Commonwealth)*
Via G. Dozza (next to the Memorial Museum of Liberty)
www.cwgc.org./admin/files/Italy.pdf

Hours: Open daily during daylight.

What to see: 184 burials. In this well-maintained cemetery, most of the headstones are inscribed with a soldier's name, unit, date of death, and age at time of death. Many also have phrases selected by the person's family. For example, one inscription reads: "In proud and everlasting memory of my dearly loved son."

Polish Cemetery *(Cimitero Polacco)*
Via G. Dozza (next to the Memorial Museum of Liberty)

Hours: Tuesday 9am–noon; Sunday 9am–11am.

What to see: Behind the entrance gate stands a lofty stone structure that shelters an altar. A cross marks each soldier's grave. The inscription on the entrance arch honors Poland's participation in the Italian campaign, where its units formed a part of the Eighth Army.

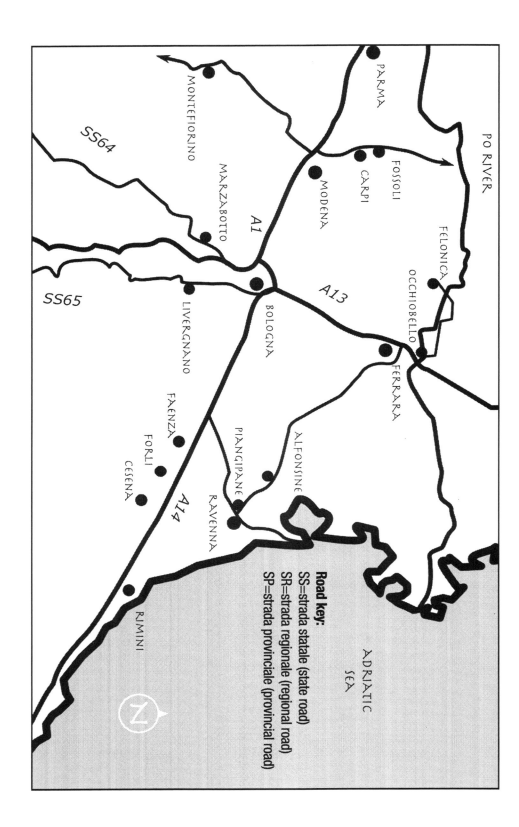

Road key:
SS=strada statale (state road)
SR=strada regionale (regional road)
SP=strada provinciale (provincial road)

Day Trips from Bologna

Travel notes: This chapter describes important sites in Bologna's region, Emilia-Romagna. Half of these locations can be reached by train or bus; for the rest you will need a car.

General tourist information in English
www.emiliaromagnaturismo.it/english/

WEST OF BOLOGNA
Deportation Memorial Museum *(Museo al Deportato)* in Carpi
Piazza dei Martiri 68, tel. 059688272

Hours: Friday, Saturday, and Sunday, 10am–1pm and 3pm–7pm.

Admission: €3

Directions: By car from Bologna, drive east on expressway A1 to the exit for expressway E45, just past the city of Modena. Take E45 to the Carpi exit and follow signs to the city center, Piazza dei Martiri (Piazza of the Martyrs). This vast piazza is named after the sixteen executed partisans whose bodies were dumped there by German troops. The museum occupies the ground floor of a historic palace bordering the piazza. Park on the

Crowds gather in Piazza dei Martiri, Carpi.
Frank J. Davis Collection, Southern Methodist University

street and walk through a large archway into a courtyard, where you will see the museum entrance.

Carpi also can be reached by train from Bologna. From the train station, walk four blocks on Viale Dallai and Corso Cabassi to Carpi's center, Piazza dei Martiri.

What to see: This museum serves as a memorial to the millions who died in concentration camps. The ticket office provides an English guide to the museum's thirteen rooms, whose walls display quotations from prisoners' letters and art work depicting camp life. Some glass cases exhibit photographs of executions and the death chambers. Others display prisoners' uniforms and identity badges. The names of 14,314 Italians who died in the camps fill the walls of the final room. Just outside the museum stand sixteen massive slabs engraved with the names of World War II concentration camps.

Deportation Camp *(Ex-Campo di Transito)* at Fossoli
Via Remesina Esterna; www.deportati.it/english_fossoli.html

Hours: *March–July*, Sundays 10am–12:30pm and 3:30am–7pm.
Other months by appointment; write to **fondazione.fossoli@carpidiem.it**.

Directions: Drive north from Carpi for four miles on Via Remesina Esterna. The camp is on the right, just past the village of Fossoli. No trains or public buses run to the camp, but you can hire a cab in Carpi.

Historical summary/what to see: In July 1942 this camp was created to hold Allied POWs, as many as five thousand during the summer of 1943. After the armistice in September 1943, the Italian guards left and the Allied prisoners escaped. The Germans then took control of the camp, using it as a holding center for Jews and political detainees. They first sent prisoners from here to Auschwitz in February 1944. Among those captives was Primo Levi, who later published several books about his wartime experiences.

Nine more transports of prisoners occurred between February and August 1944, when the Allied advance caused the Germans to close the camp. Its inmates were transferred to a holding center near the Austrian border. After World War II, the camp at Fossoli served as a shelter for political refugees and other groups until 1970.

Most of the camp's buildings are dilapidated, although their foundations and some walls still remain. Local craftsmen have restored several structures; one serves as an exhibit hall. Posted there are maps of the camp's original plan. The maps indicate that Jewish prisoners occupied eight barracks, while political detainees filled another seven. Barbed wire separated those two groups of barracks from each other and from the Germans' quarters.

Cervi Museum and Institute
(Museo Cervi e Istituto Alcide Cervi) near Parma
Via Cervi 9, Gattatico (near Parma), tel. 0522678356; www.fratellicervi.it

Hours: Daily except Mondays: *April–September*, 9am–1pm and 3pm–7pm;
October–March, 9am–12:30pm and 3pm–5:30pm.

Directions: From Carpi or Bologna, take expressway A1 west toward Parma. Exit at the sign for "Terre di Canossa-Campegine" and follow signs for the museum.

Historical summary/what to see: This museum honors the family of Alcide and Genoveffa Cervi, who had seven sons and two daughters. The sons, like their father, were farmers, and all seven were active in the Resistance. German soldiers arrested the Cervi sons on November 25, 1943, took them to a prison in Reggio Emilia, and executed them on December 28, 1943. After the war, the family's house became a place of pilgrimage. In the 1960s, the property began its transformation into a center for twentieth-century history, with a focus on the Cervi family, the Resistance, and the role of agriculture in the rebirth of Italy after the war.

Museum of the Partisan Republic
(Museo della Repubblica Partigiana) in Montefiorino
Via Rocca 1, tel. 0536954139

Hours: *July–August*, Tuesday–Sunday 10am–12:30pm and 3pm–6:30pm. *September–June*, Sunday only, same hours

Directions: Montefiorino is south of the city of Modena and is easy to visit on the way to Carpi or the Cervi Museum (described above). Take expressway A1 to the exit for SS486 and follow signs for Montefiorino.

What to see: This handsome museum is in a medieval fortress in the village center. It exhibits documents, photographs, and artifacts that tell (in Italian) the story of local partisan brigades.

SITES NEAR OR IN MARZABOTTO
The History Park of Monte Sole *(Parco Storico di Monte Sole)*
Tel. 051932525; www.montesole.org (click on British flag for an English version; the website also describes a school associated with the park).

Hours: Allow at least half a day to visit the History Park, which is best seen during daylight. If you have several days to spend, consider staying in the modest lodgings offered by Il Poggiolo, a hotel within the park's reception center. Booking information is given in the Hotels section.

Directions: From Bologna, take SS64 to Pian de Venola, a village next to the town of Marzabotto. Turn left at the signs for "Monte Sole," "Il Poggiolo," and "Scuola di Pace." Follow the road up the mountain to a parking lot near two large buildings, one of which is the park's reception center. The other hosts a Peace School (Scuola di Pace) related to the park.

Historical summary: In the mountains south of Bologna in the summer of 1944, German troops and Italian Fascists were rounding up young men to serve in forced labor camps or Mussolini's army. In response, bands of Italian partisans were attacking German truck convoys, derailing trains, and killing soldiers. As many as twelve hundred partisans were engaged in guerrilla warfare against the Germans in the Marzabotto area, which includes the mountain called Monte Sole.

As partisan activity increased, German commanders announced that they would arrest and execute not only partisans, but also a percentage of the civilians in areas where partisan groups gathered. At first the Germans punished or executed small numbers of civilians as part of their campaign of reprisal and intimidation. When partisans continued their assaults, German commanders decided to carry out a more deadly attack, in part to gain control of Monte Sole as a defense against the advancing Allies.

On September 29, 1944, about fifteen hundred German soldiers encircled the villages on Monte Sole and began the killing spree. Over the next few days, they used machine guns and hand grenades to execute somewhere between seven hundred and twelve hundred people. Many of the victims were women, children, and infants.

Most of the buildings damaged or destroyed during this raid were abandoned and fell into ruin. In the late 1980s, the government of Emilia Romagna turned Monte Sole and its surroundings into a memorial park. Today the remains of churches and houses bear silent witness to what happened here. More details about this horrific event are given below and in journalist Jack Olsen's book, *Silence on Monte Sole.*

What to see: From the reception center, winding roads lead to the sites where Italian civilians were massacred. These locations are easy to find by following posted signs. At selected points on the itinerary, panels provide additional information in Italian.

To reach the first site, a church, walk several hundred yards past the Peace School and turn right at the junction of two roads. Signs point to the ruins of the church of San Martino, which until 1944 served about sixty families. On September 30, 1944, fifty villagers took refuge in this church. The German soldiers forced them to leave and executed everyone in front of a nearby house. After the massacre, the church was abandoned.

From San Martino, return to the junction of two roads. Follow signs to the remains of several settlements. The first, less than a mile from the junction, is Caprara, which once bustled with life. Here German soldiers herded fifty women and children into a room and killed them with hand grenades. Still farther down the road are the ruins of Casaglia. In its cemetery German troops executed eighty villagers.

From Casaglia's cemetery a narrow road leads to Cerpiano, where before the war there were several substantial houses. On September 29, fifty women and children hid in one of these houses, but were discovered and forced into the nearby chapel. German troops then closed the doors and killed almost everyone with hand grenades. Miraculously, three people survived that assault, but in the following days hundreds more civilians were murdered in the area of Monte Sole.

This killing spree was the most deadly of those carried out in Italy during the war, but not the only one. For example, on March 24, 1944, German soldiers executed 335 men at the Ardeatine Caves in Rome (see Chapter 5). In August 1944, they slaughtered hundreds of civilians at Sant'Anna, a village near Lucca (see Chapter 8).

The History Park is open throughout the year and hosts the Peace School, whose mission is to promote intercultural understanding. Its programs serve students from Italy, other

European countries, and the Middle East. To learn more, visit **www.sitesofconscience.org**.

Memorial Chapel *(Sacrario ai Caduti)*

Hours: Daily except Monday: *May 16–September 30,* 9am–12:15pm and 3pm–5:15pm; *October 1–May 15,* 9am–11:45am and 2pm–4:45pm.

Directions: By car from the History Park, take SS64 (also called Via Porrettana) north for a few miles to the center of Marzabotto. Park near its one large church (marked by a tall spire) and enter the chapel through the gate that surrounds the back of the church.

The chapel also can be reached by thirty-minute train ride from Bologna. Exit at the Marzabotto station and make your first right. Walk one block to the corner, where a small grocery store stands on the right. Turn left, walk a block to the church with the lofty spire, and enter the chapel through the gate that surrounds the back of the church.

What to see: Here rest the remains of 782 local citizens killed by German soldiers between September 28 and October 1, 1944; see above for the details of this massacre. The victims who could be identified lie in the chapel's burial recesses. Those who could not be identified were placed in three marble tombs. Paintings and other works of art adorn the chapel's interior walls. Behind the altar, frescoes depict partisans going to and returning from battle. The central fresco portrays Christ embracing a partisan's family. At the other end of the chapel, wall panels show women mourning for their husbands and rejoicing at the rebirth of liberty.

The niches along the chapel's side walls also contain works of art that depict wartime events. The scenes are labeled, making interpretation easier. *La vedetta partigiana* (the partisan lookout) depicts a person watching for signs of danger. *Soccorso al ferito* (aid to the wounded) portrays a woman caring for an injured man. *Morte dell'innocente* (death of an innocent) depicts a woman mourning her dead baby. *Il dolore* (suffering) shows a woman being burned to death.

The government of Italy awarded gold medals for military valor to four local men. Their actions are described on plaques near the chapel's main door. The first plaque praises Francesco Calzolari, a partisan leader executed by the Germans in June 1944. The second honors Gastone Rossi, a sixteen-year old partisan who saved his comrades by throwing himself on a bomb. The third commends Mario Musolesi, the commander of the Stella Rossa brigade. The fourth lauds a local priest, Don Giovanni Fornasini, who tried to protect his parishioners and openly criticized German officials for the massacre. He was executed by the Germans on October 13, 1944.

National Etruscan Museum "Pompeo Aria" *(Museo Nazionale Etrusco)* in Marzabotto
www.archeobo.arti.beniculturali.it/Marzabotto/note_en.htm

Hours: Museum: *April–October,* daily except Monday, 9am–1pm and 3pm–6:30pm; *November–March,* same days, 9am–1pm and 2pm–5:30pm. The town is open daily 8am–7pm. Both sites are closed May 1, December 25, and January 1.

Admission: Museum €2; free to the town

Directions: The ruins of this Etruscan settlement have no connection to the war, but are worth seeing if you have time. As you leave the memorial chapel, turn right and walk a block to the corner, where a sign points to "Zona Archaeologica" (Archaeological Zone). Turn left at that sign and follow the sidewalk along the highway for ten minutes (on foot) to the entrance. For those who prefer to drive, there is ample parking.

What to see: The museum exhibits artifacts found at this site and provides a brochure in English that describes the ancient town's buildings, streets, and graveyards. Etruscan settlers built huts here as early as the sixth century BCE. They established a town in the fifth century BCE; its streets and some building foundations remain. The ruins stand on a scenic bluff overlooking the Reno River, one of many rivers that Allied troops crossed as they advanced north.

TWO MUSEUMS
Winter Line Museum *(Museo "Winter Line")* in Livergnano
Via della Chiesa 4, tel. 3805074820

Hours: Sunday 2pm–5pm; weekdays by appointment.

Directions: The village of Livergnano is about nineteen miles south of Bologna on SS65, a highway used for the Allied advance. If you do not have a car, contact the museum in advance to request a weekday visit, when there is limited bus service from Bologna.

Historical summary/what to see: This small museum is named after the German defensive line that crossed this rugged area. Livergnano sits on a rocky ridge about five thousand feet high and almost three miles long. In the fall of 1944, German troops held these heights; the remains of their bunkers are still visible on paths from the village. In October 1944, Fifth Army forces suffered heavy casualties while fighting to take Livergnano and mountains south of that village. Allied pilots subsequently bombed German positions; those bombardments and renewed infantry attacks forced the Germans to retreat from Livergnano. The Fifth Army offensive ended in late 1944, when troops entered winter quarters, and resumed in the spring of 1945.

The museum fills a space created by carving into the rock ridge. It displays artifacts that German and American soldiers left in this area, such as coins, ration boxes, cigarette wrappers, gloves, boots, radio transmitters, weapons, and shovels. The museum owners, Umberto and Patrizia Magnani, have welcomed visitors here for many years. In 2002, a woman from Massachusetts mentioned that her father had died from wounds received at Livergnano. After recalling that the museum had a flask engraved with her father's last name and the words "Italy" and "Mass," Mr. Magnani gave this flask to the soldier's daughter.

About a mile south of Livergnano on SS65 stands a monument to the 361st Regiment of the U.S. 91st Division. A small park in the nearby town of Loiano contains a memorial to the 362nd Regiment of the U.S. 91st Division. Both regiments fought in this area.

Wounded and dead German soldiers near the Po River, April 1945.
Frank J. Davis Collection, Southern Methodist University

World War II Museum of the Po River *(Museo della Seconda Guerra Mondiale del Fiume Po)* in Felonica

Piazza Municipio 15, tel. 038666180; www.museofelonica.it

Hours: Monday–Friday 9am–noon; Sunday and holidays 3pm–6pm.

Admission: €5

Directions: By car, take expressway A14 toward Padova (Padua). Exit at Occhiobello and follow signs for Mantova and Ostigilia. Go through the village of Gaiba and follows signs to the left for Bondeno. After you cross the Po, follow signs to the right for the town of Felonica. The museum entrance is on the right side of town hall, a centrally-located large stucco building with ample parking. Alternatively, take the train to Felonica from Bologna.

Historical summary/what to see: The museum's exhibits concern the weeks between the liberation of Bologna (April 21, 1945) and the end of the war in May. During that time, the Fifth and Eighth Armies linked up and continued their pursuit of German forces, thousands of whom were taken prisoner. Germans not yet captured hurried north through the flatlands to the Po River, where they found the bridges destroyed. Abandoning their heavy weapons, cases, and vehicles, they swam or took rowboats across the river. The museum displays samples of the equipment left by German soldiers on the banks of the Po as they fled north, such as weapons, gas cans, portable stoves, medical kits, and saddles. It also exhibits well-chosen photos of Allied and Axis forces engaged in action near the Po.

In contrast to the Germans, the Allies used bridging equipment to bring their troops across the river. The museum director can provide directions to the monuments that mark the Allied crossings of the Po.

RAVENNA AREA

Eighth Army troops liberated Ravenna in December 1944. However, German forces held Alfonsine and other towns near Ravenna until April 1945. Prior to that month, the Germans had fortified the banks of the Senio River (which flows through Alfonsine) with tunnels and bunkers. After Allied pilots bombed those defenses, Eighth Army units began their assault at dusk on April 9. By April 11, those troops fought their way to the Santerno River, almost four miles from the Senio. For gallantry in battle, two Indian Army soldiers were awarded the Victoria Cross, the British Commonwealth's highest military decoration.

Museum of the Battle of the Senio *(Museo della Battaglia del Senio)* in Alfonsine

Piazza della Resistenza 2, tel. 054484302; www.romagnadeste.it/en

Hours: *June–July and September–March,* Monday–Friday 9am–noon and 2pm–5pm. *April–May*, same weekday hours, also open weekends 9am–noon and 3pm–6pm.

Directions/what to see: From Bologna, take expressway A14 east. Just past the town of Imola, exit at the sign for Ravenna. Drive fifteen miles northeast and exit at the sign for SS (State Road) 16, which runs to Alfonsine. Alternatively, take the train from Bologna to Ravenna and change there for Alfonsine, only fifteen minutes by train from Ravenna. Follow signs to the war museum, which stands a block from the train station. Its collection contains photographs, flags, weapons, and other materials that document the activities of partisans and Allied forces in this area.

Villanova Canadian War Cemetery *(Commonwealth)*

www.cwgc.org./admin/files/Italy.pdf

Hours: Open daily during daylight.

Directions/what to see: 212 burials. From Alfonsine, drive southbound on SS16 to the village of Mezzano. From there, follow signs for two miles to the village of Villanova; the cemetery is on its outskirts. The men buried here died in the battles at Ravenna or along the Senio River. Most of the headstones are inscribed with a soldier's name, unit, date of death, and age at time of death. The graves of those who could not be identified note the burial of a soldier "known unto God."

Gunners of the Royal Artillery (Eighth Army) near Ravenna, February 1945.
Library and Archives Canada

Italian Military Cemetery *(Sacrario Militare)* at Camerlona

Directions/what to see: Return to SS16 and drive south for about two miles to the village of Camerlona. There follow signs for the cemetery, which is adorned by marble buildings and a large cross. Buried here are soldiers of the Combat Group "Cremona," one of the first divisions of the Italian Co-Belligerent Army. That army was formed by Italian soldiers and officers after its predecessor, the Royal Italian Army, fell apart in 1943. From 1943 until the spring of 1945, Italian units supported the Allies in zones behind the front. At the battle along the Senio River, the Combat Group "Cremona" fought on the front lines.

Ravenna War Cemetery *(Commonwealth)*

www.cwgc.org./admin/files/Italy.pdf

Hours: Open daily during daylight.

What to see: 955 burials. From Camerlona, follow signs west for a few miles to the village of Piangipane. The men buried here died in battles at Ravenna or along the Senio River. Eighth Army troops from Canada, New Zealand, and India lie here, as well as thirty-three soldiers of the Jewish Infantry Brigade. That unit was formed in 1944; its soldiers came chiefly from Palestine.

Trieste

Travel notes: Trieste has two national memorials: La Risiera, a former death camp that is now a major museum, and the Foiba Monument, where victims of the war are buried. The city also possesses a spectacular waterfront setting on the Adriatic and excellent museums. Visitors interested in the career of James Joyce may visit where he lived and worked. By train, Trieste is four hours from Bologna and ninety minutes from Venice.

General tourist information in English: www.turismo.fvg.it

Historical summary: Trieste has a long and complex history. Founded as a Roman colony before the birth of Christ, it was governed by Austria from the fourteenth century until the end of World War I, when Italy took control of Trieste. However, Italian governance did not end questions about the city's identity. Trieste still stood at the junction of two nations with different languages and cultures: Italy and Yugoslavia (which then included Slovenes, Croatians, and other groups). Although most residents of Trieste spoke Italian as their first language, the majority of those living in the area around the city spoke Slovene or Croat as their first language.

When Mussolini and the Fascist Party came to power in Italy, they mistreated the Yugoslav population in Trieste and its surrounding region. The Fascists forced some Yugoslavs to move from their lands and organized a broad "Italianization" project that sought, for example, to suppress the use of Slavic languages in Trieste's region. Slavic-language schools in Trieste were closed. This harsh treatment helped to foster the growth of the Yugoslav resistance movement. To destroy that movement, Mussolini ordered Italian forces to burn Yugoslav villages and execute partisans. When Mussolini was deposed in July 1943, Yugoslav partisans took their revenge by killing hundred of Italians and throwing their bodies into deep pits (*foibe*) near Trieste.

In September 1943, German forces occupied Trieste. As elsewhere in Italy, the Germans took over government buildings and tried to suppress partisan groups. They also set up and helped to run Italy's only death camp and crematorium, the remains of which have been turned into a national memorial site.

By the fall of 1944, with Germany on the brink of defeat, it was becoming clear that the Soviet Union wanted to control Eastern Europe after the war. The Soviets' ambitions worried British and American leaders, as did these events: the Russian army's rapid advance to the west, the liberation of eastern Yugoslavia by Tito's Communist troops, and Tito's treaty of friendship with Russia, signed in mid-April, 1945.

To rein in the Communists, Eighth Army troops (the Second New Zealand Division) were sent to Trieste in late April 1945. Those forces arrived on May 2, one day after the arrival of Yugoslav troops. The Germans holding the Castle of San Giusto surrendered to the New Zealanders. A joint attack by Yugoslav and New Zealand units forced German troops in the Palace of Justice to surrender.

General William Gentry, the commander of Eighth Army troops in Trieste, set up his headquarters in a hotel on the harbor. His quarters were just around the corner from those of the Yugoslav commander in Piazza dell'Unità, Trieste's largest and most beautiful square. The simultaneous presence of two military forces that were technically allies, but in reality competitors, made it difficult to bring peace to Trieste. Both Yugoslav and Allied commanders claimed the right to manage Trieste and its region, but their political philosophies had nothing in common: the Yugoslavs advocated Communism, while the Allies pressed for democracy.

To further complicate matters, local political parties differed on the question of which nation should govern Trieste after the war. The city's Communists were eager for Yugoslavia to control Trieste, but the city's pro-democracy parties argued that first the Allies and then Italy should govern Trieste and its region.

In May 1945, Yugoslav military leaders tried to push Allied personnel out of Trieste and its region, but did not succeed. The postwar Allied government joined with pro-democracy Italian organizations to thwart Yugoslav plans. In June 1945, after weeks of negotiation, the two sides agreed to divide the disputed area into two zones. They assigned Zone A, which included Trieste, to the Allies. Zone B was assigned to Yugoslav civilian and military control. In 1954, Trieste and most of Zone A were put under Italian control, and the city today is firmly a part of Italy.

ON THE OUTSKIRTS OF TRIESTE
Civic Museum of the San Sabba Risiera
(Civico Museo della Risiera di San Sabba)
Via Giovanni Palatucci 5 or Ratto della Pileria 43, tel. 040826202; www.jewishitaly.org

Hours: Daily 9am–7pm; closed January 1 and December 25.

Directions: From Piazza Unità d'Italia, the center of Trieste, take bus #10 (its final stop, Piazza Valmaura, is printed on the front of the bus). Ask the driver to stop at La Risiera, a trip of about fifteen minutes. After exiting the bus, cross the street (Via Rio) and walk a block down Via Giovanni Palatucci to the museum's imposing entrance. The stark thirty-five-foot walls that flank this site's entrance were erected after the war. The architect designed them to create an atmosphere expressive of the horrors that occurred here.

By car, take SS (State Road) 202 to the exit for "Valmaura/Stadio"and follow signs for La Risiera. Parking is available on the street.

What to see: In October 1943, the German occupiers turned this former rice factory into a prison for the detention, interrogation, and execution of their enemies. Many of the buildings used for those purposes still stand in a cluster around a central courtyard. La Risiera also served as a transit center for Jews and others marked for deportation to death camps in Germany or Poland.

In March 1944, the Germans set up a crematorium in the center of La Risiera. The following month, the first cremations of executed prisoners were carried out. It is estimated that between three thousand and five thousand people were killed here; of that number, many were Slovenes. On April 29, 1945, the Germans dynamited the crematorium to remove evidence of their crimes and then fled.

As visitors walk down the somber entranceway, they arrive first at an office that sells books and pamphlets in English and other languages. Next to that office is a large room called the "death cell," which held prisoners marked for execution within a few hours. This space was also used to store bodies awaiting cremation.

Next to the death cell is a larger room that contains seventeen closet-size cells, each equipped with a bunk bed made of planks. The first two closet-size cells were used for torture and storage of property taken from the prisoners. Items found there included identity papers now preserved in the Archive of the Slovenian Republic. The remaining small cells held people who were to be executed within a few days or weeks. Graffitti used to cover the walls; those writings have faded. However, the scholar Diego de Henriquez copied the graffiti into his diaries, which are kept at the Trieste museum that bears his name.

The floors above the cells housed offices, dormitories, and the workshops where prisoners made clothing and shoes. The adjacent four-story building likewise contained dormitories, workshops, and storage. In the courtyard, only yards from the prisoners' quarters, stood a one-story building that covered the underground cremation oven. The Germans destroyed that building at the end of the war, and its area is now marked by a large metal plate. An underground passageway connected the oven and its chimney stack. The chimney's base now serves as a platform for a sculpture that represents the smoke that came from the crematorium.

On one side of the courtyard stands a six-story building. During the war, the upper floors served as barracks for German, Austrian, and Ukrainian troops. Its ground floor, formerly a kitchen and dining hall, now hosts a museum that displays artwork, photographs, Holocaust relics, and objects stolen from local Jews during the war. The notes explaining these items are in six languages, including English. The museum also shows a documentary with English subtitles.

Behind the museum is a chapel/exhibit hall that served as a garage for military vehicles during the occupation.

Foiba Monument at Basovizza *(Foiba di Basovizza)*

Hours: *July–February*, daily 10am–4pm; *March–June*, daily 10am–6pm.

Directions: The village of Basovizza is a twenty-minute bus ride north of Trieste. Take bus #39 from Via Carducci 5 (near Piazza Oberdan) or from the train station. Tell the driver that you are going to the "Foiba" and he/she will let you off at the closest stop, which is in front of a school on Via Igo Gruden in Basovizza. After exiting the bus, walk left for one block through the village's commercial district, which has signs written in Italian and Slovenian. Take your first right on Via Dragotin Kette. Walk one block to a two-lane paved road. Signs there point to "Foiba." Go across that road to a one-lane street and walk for ten minutes to the memorial site, which is circled by a low stone wall. If you drive from Trieste, ample parking is available.

What to see: Like La Risiera, the Foiba site is a national monument. It commemorates the Italians slain by Yugoslav partisans after Mussolini was deposed (summer 1943) and in May–June 1945. Those partisans were seeking revenge for their sufferings under Italian Fascists and trying to facilitate a Communist takeover of Italy in the postwar period. The word *foiba* (plural *foibe*) means "pit" in English.

This site has seven memorials and a small museum that displays wartime photographs accompanied by historical summaries in Italian. One panel tells the story of Norma Cossetto, a local girl who was raped, killed, and buried in the pit. Another panel lists the names of sixteen other villages near Trieste where pits were used to dispose of bodies. The museum also sells English-language books and pamphlets about these executions.

Outside the museum, a massive metal square now covers the pit where bodies were placed. From after the war until 1959, this pit was used as a dump. In 1961, a temporary cover was installed. The current cover was put in place in 2006 and is circled by seven bronze or stone memorials, whose inscriptions are translated (or summarized) below in sequence:

- The memorial nearest the pit has a chart listing what was found during postwar excavations. At a depth of 256 meters, the excavators found World War I cannons; at 228 meters, the bodies of people executed during World War II; at 198 meters, World War II munitions; at 135 meters, trash.
- The second monument's inscription means: "Honor and Christian compassion to those who died. May their sacrifice remind men of the ways of justice and love, through which flourishes true peace."
- The third memorial is dedicated to combatants killed in May and June 1945; it notes that Trieste, after undergoing a "very harsh occupation by foreign powers, endured with dignity the martyrdom of the killings and the pits, and did not refuse to show actively its attachment to the fatherland."
- The fourth commemorates Italian mountain troops, called Alpini in Italian.
- The fifth and sixth honor ninety-seven members of the Italian military body that investigates financial crimes.
- The seventh recognizes Italian policemen buried here.

IN THE CENTER OF TRIESTE
The Great Synagogue (*Tempio Maggiore*)
At the junction of Via San Francesco and Via Donizetti, tel. 0406371466; www.jewishitaly.org

Hours: Guided tours are given in English on Sunday at 10am, 11am, and noon, and on Wednesdays at 3:30pm, 4:30pm, and 5:30 pm.

Admission: €3.50

Directions/what to see: This vast synagogue is three blocks from Piazza Oberdan and a block from the Palace of Justice, a building held by the Germans during the occupation. Frescoes, mosaics, and stained glass windows adorn this splendid house of worship, which the occupiers had planned to use as a museum or swimming pool. The guide discusses the history of the synagogue and the Jewish community in Trieste. Services are held here on a regular basis.

Carlo and Vera Wagner Museum of the Jewish Community (*Museo della Comunità Ebraica*)

Via del Monte 5–7, tel. 040633819; www.jewishitaly.org

Hours: Sunday 5pm–8pm; Tuesday 4pm–7pm; Thursday 10am–1pm.

Admission: €5.5

Directions/what to see: This museum stands on the street between Piazza Benco and the grand staircase leading to Castle San Giusto (described below). It exhibits precious textiles, silver objects, books, and other artifacts related to Jewish family life and synagogue rituals. Some of these items were hidden in Trieste's synagogue during the occupation.

Castle of San Giusto (*Castello di San Giusto*)

Via San Giusto

Hours: *April–October*, daily 9am–7pm; *November–March*, daily 9am–5pm.

Admission: €5

Directions/what to see: Take public bus #24 or the scenic pedestrian route uphill to this fifteenth-century castle, which sits on a hill overlooking the city and harbor. Near the castle stands a dramatic Fascist-era monument erected in 1933 to honor Italian soldiers killed in World War I. At the end of World War II, German troops barricaded themselves in the castle before surrendering to New Zealand forces here. Today the castle hosts an archaeology museum as well as a collection of historic armor and weapons. Near the castle's entrance stand some of Trieste's impressive Roman ruins and the Cathedral of San Giusto.

Endnotes

1. Newby, *Love and War in the Apennines*, 48.
2. Atkinson, *Day of Battle*, 240.
3. Pyle, *Brave Men*, 151.
4. Atkinson, *Day of Battle*, 345–50.
5. Corti, *Last Soldiers*, 248.
6. Pyle, *Brave Men*, 254-5.
7. Taney, *Fighting 36th Quarterly*, 78.
8. Atkinson, *Day of Battle*, 395.
9. Katz, *Battle for Rome*, 17.
10. Scrivener, *Inside Rome*, 6.
11. Scrivener, *Inside Rome*, 177.
12. Ridley, *Mussolini*, 225.
13. Orgill, *Gothic Line*, 128.
14. Orgill, *Gothic Line*, 120.
15. Speer, quoted by Orgill, *Gothic Line*, 128–9.
16. Orgill, *Gothic Line*, 168.
17. Fisher, *Cassino to the Alps*, 328.
18. Holland, *Italy's Sorrow*, 431.
19. Ellis, *See Naples and Die*, 125.

Bibliography

Adelman, Robert H., and George Walton. *The Devil's Brigade.*
 Philadelphia: Chilton Books, 1966.

Atkinson, Rick. *The Day of Battle: The War in Sicily and Italy, 1943-1944.*
 New York: Henry Holt, 2007.

Ballinger, Pamela. *History in Exile: Memory and Identity at the Borders of the Balkans.*
 Princeton: Princeton University Press, 2003.

Blumenson, Martin. *The United States Army in World War II: Salerno to Cassino.*
 Washington DC: Office of the Chief of Military History, United States Army, 1969.

Bosworth, R. J. B. *Mussolini.* London: Hodder Arnold, 2002.

Brooks, Thomas. *The War North of Rome: June 1944–May 1945.*
 New York: Sarpedon, 1996.

Corti, Eugenio. *The Last Soldiers of the King.* Translated by Manuela Arundel.
 Columbia: University of Missouri Press, 2003.

Cox, Geoffrey. *The Race for Trieste.* London: William Kimber, 1977.

Delzell, Charles F. *Mussolini's Enemies: The Italian Anti-Fascist Resistance.*
 New York: Howard Fertig, 1974.

Ellis, Robert B. *See Naples and Die: A World War II Memoir of a United States Army
 Ski Trooper in the Mountains of Italy.* Jefferson, NC: McFarland, 1996.

D'Este, Carlo. *Fatal Decision: Anzio and the Battle for Rome.*
 New York: Harper Collins, 1991.

Fisher, Ernest F. *The United States Army in World War II: Cassino to the Alps.*
 Washington DC: Center of Military History, United States Army, 1977.

Gooderson, Ian. *Cassino.* London: Brassey's, 2003.

Holland, James. *Italy's Sorrow: A Year of War, 1944–1945.*
 New York: St. Martin's Press, 2008.

Hoyt, Edwin P. *Backwater War: The Allied Campaign in Italy, 1943-1945.*
 Westport, CT: Praeger, 2002.

Huebner, Claus K. *Long Walk through War: A Combat Doctor's Diary.*
 College Station: Texas A&M University Press, 1987.

Katz, Robert. *The Battle for Rome: The Germans, the Allies, the Partisans, and the Pope.*
 New York: Simon and Schuster, 2003.

Lewis, Norman. *Naples '44.* New York: Pantheon, 1978.

McBride, James. *Miracle at St. Anna.* New York: Riverhead, 2001.

Murphy, Audie. 1949. *To Hell and Back.* New York: Henry Holt, 2002.

Newby, Eric. 1971. *Love and War in the Apennines.* New York: Penguin, 1990.

Novak, Bogdan C. *Trieste, 1941–1954.* Chicago: University of Chicago Press, 1970.

Olsen, Jack. *Silence on Monte Sole.* New York: G. P. Putnam, 1968.

Origo, Iris. *War in Val d'Orcia: An Italian War Diary, 1943-1944.*
 London: Jonathan Cape, 1947.

Orgill, Douglas. *The Gothic Line.* London: William Heinemann, 1967.

Paticchia, Vito, and Paolo Zurzolo. *Percorsi della Memoria, 1940–1945: La Storia, I Luoghi.* Bologna: Clueb, 2005.

Paticchia, Vito, et al. *Emilia Romagna: A Journey into the Region's Wartime Past.* Milan: Touring Editore, 2005.

Portelli, Alessandro. *The Order Has Been Carried Out: History, Memory and Meaning of a Nazi Massacre in Rome.* New York: Palgrave Macmillan, 2003.

Pugliese, Stanislao. *Desperate Inscriptions: Graffiti from the Nazi Prisons in Rome, 1943–1944.* Boca Raton: Bordighera, 2002.

Ridley, Jasper. *Mussolini: A Biography.* New York: Cooper Square Press, 2000.

Starr, Chester. *From Salerno to the Alps.* Washington DC: Infantry Journal Press, 1948.

Taney, Warren. *The Fighting 36th Historical Quarterly* (Spring 1989): 76–80.

Tompkins, Peter. *Italy Betrayed.* New York: Simon and Schuster, 1966.

Tregaskis, Richard. *Invasion Diary.* New York: Random House, 1944.

Tutaev, David. *The Consul of Florence.* London: Secker & Marburg, 1966.

Wilhelm, Maria de Blasio. *The Other Italy: Italian Resistance in World War II.* New York: Norton, 1988.

Wyss, M. de. *Rome under the Terror.* London: Robert Hale, 1945.

Zimmerman, Joshua D., ed. *Jews in Italy under Fascist and Nazi Rule, 1922-1945.* Cambridge: Cambridge University Press, 2005.

Selected Films

The Battle of San Pietro (1945)
Rome, Open City (1945)
The Story of G.I. Joe (1945)
A Walk in the Sun (1945)
Paisan (1946)
Tragic Pursuit (1947)
Bitter Rice (1948)
Darby's Rangers (1958)
The Four Days of Naples (1962)
Anzio (1968)
The Devil's Brigade (1968)
Patton (1970)
The Night of San Lorenzo (1982)
A War of Their Own: Canadians in Italy and Sicily (2000)

About the Author

Anne Saunders is a Research Associate in the Classics Department at the College of Charleston, where she taught Latin literature for twenty-two years. Her other publications include journal articles and translations of Latin poetry and prose. In recent years her work has focused on World War II Italy. She holds a BA from Wellesley College, a MA from Columbia University, and a PhD from the University of South Carolina.

Made in the USA
Lexington, KY
01 July 2012